Be Not Afraid
It Is I

"A Supernatural Walk Through Childbirth"

By Nancy Dignan

Be Not Afraid, It is I
A Supernatural Walk Through Childbirth" John 6:20

© 2003 by Nancy Dignan

ISBN-13: 978-1499785296
ISBN-10: 1499785291

First printing 2011
Second Printing 2014
Printed in the UnitedStates of America
Firestarter Publications 120 Glade Place, Dover, AR 72837

The names of the individuals in these stories have been changed to protect their identity. The scriptural references have been taken from various translations of the Bible such as Amplified New Testament © Zondervan Corporation 1975, New King James Version © Thomas Nelson Inc. 1982

The Books and Authors mentioned in this book do not constitute their agreement or support of the content of this book. It is the expressed desire of the author to allow this book to be reproduced in any form. Also that any quotations would not be taken out of context and all would be for the Glory of the Lord Jesus Christ. Any Comments may be posted on Firestarterpublications.com

Contents

Chapter		Page
	Forward	4
1.	Vision	6
2	.Fearfully and Wonderfully Made	10
3.	Knowledge of Him	13
4.	Love	16
5.	Faith	20
6.	Faith Like This	24
7.	Living in The Promises	27
8.	Father. Mother and Child	33
9.	Waiting	39
10.	Priorities	44
11.	Anointing	47
12.	God's Keeping Power	51
13.	Praise and Worship	53
14.	The Battle	57
15.	Trust	61
16.	Surrender	65
17.	Overcoming Fear	68
18.	Imaginations	74
19.	Impossible for Man	80
20.	Intercession	83
21.	Joy	87
22.	Peace	90
23.	The Suddenly of God	92
24.	The Bad Report	96
25.	The Lie	98
26.	The Lion's Den	102
27.	Laughter	105
28.	All of Creation Groans	108
29.	Casting Down Idols	112
30.	Count it all Joy	115
31.	Asleep	119
32.	Overdue Babies	122
33.	Birth Stories	124
34.	Newborn Care	142
35.	Scriptures for Strength	147
	Glossary	158

Forward

Everything in this book is an expression of my experience, yet in it I want all the glory to go to the Lord. In every thought, He is there. In every birth He is there. In every breath He is there. He has made a way for each experience and person in this book. It is His awesomeness that prompted the writing of these thoughts and experiences. I had to tell someone of His Greatness, His care for us, and His eternal wisdom which confounds the wise and causes me to look foolish. I have questioned my calling many times in 30 years but He always assures me that I must; *continue in well doing thus silencing the foolish and ignorant man. 1 Peter 2:15*

God is our Creator and He wants to teach us how to walk in faith and love with His creation. Sometimes people ask me why I would be so foolish to get up at all hours of the day and night to forge flood waters, snow, cold, and dark to put aside my plans and leisure time to go to a birth. What does it mean? I love to answer this. He is the reason. I will get to see God.

His angels, crowd in the room and joy is everywhere. Strength is there and when I close my eyes, He is there in majesty and beauty. Sometimes I forget that He is there and something will remind me like just arriving at a birth of a first time mom and maybe having some apprehension about how she will do. I go to check her to see how much time we have and much to my amazement she is complete and ready to push. She's not in pain. She's still expecting to be early and yet I get a big smile on my face and tears begin to come and I praise God thanking Him for His eternal goodness. Anointing follows those moments and great joy. Sometimes we all shout when I tell her and her husband the good news that they are going to have the baby real soon and isn't God good. We all know it is the Lord. Such strength it gives us. Sometimes the mother doesn't believe me and I don't believe myself and I check her again. The amazement on her face is worth getting out of a warm bed. Oh how good God is.

But, now thus saith the Lord that created thee, O Jacob, and he that formed thee, O Israel. Fear not: for I have redeemed thee. I have called thee by thy name, thou art mine. Isaiah. 43:1

We are redeemed. Now what does that mean? It means being saved by grace, forever in His Presence. When you love the Lord Jesus, every promise of God is yours, that is your redemption. You are the redeemed of the Lord! Say So!! I pray you are encouraged and strengthened by these words in Isaiah 41:6 *They helped every one his neighbor; and every one said to his brother. Be of good courage.*

Enjoy this journey of faith and redemption. I pray you will see the Father and walk closer to Him. I want to thank the Lord Jesus for this crazy life he has given me and for always being there and never leaving me nor forsaking me in times of trouble. I want to thank my dear husband for his never failing love and sacrifice to me, always ready to listen and pray, all the nights he waited up for me, he makes my life so happy. I want to thank my children, Todd and Joel and their families for being born and all the joy and fun they are in my life. To Jeanne Saul for helping me with this book and making it so easy. To my Dad who always wanted to hear my stories and then begged me to write them down. To my mother who is such a wonderful inspiration to me. To all the families who have let me be a part of their family. To all my friends who encouraged me to write to other families to encourage them. Thanks to all my fellow midwives, God bless you all. Thank you, dear ones. I love you!

> I give all my Praise to the King
> Maker of everything
> Love unending, beauty and grace
> Merciful King I give you Praise
> Merciful King I give you Praise!!

Chapter 1

The Vision

My journey starts with the birth of my first son, Todd. What a shock. I am pregnant. How could this happen, I wasn't planning a baby? Now what do I do? I always babysat and loved children but I never really thought I would have any children until I was told I was pregnant. A whole new world opened up for me.

We had moved to Green Bay, Wisconsin and I didn't know anyone. We were not near family so I just did the best I could. My husband was working a lot so I did all the doctor visits by myself. I can't say I was scared because I didn't have enough information to be. I used to hear the saying, "ignorance is bliss", but I really believe that is a lie. I got really excited about baby Todd. I always knew it was Todd and never even considered what if it wasn't.

One snowy night in November my labor started. I was shocked at how it hurt. I called the doctor immediately and he said to come in right away. The contractions were 5 minutes apart. The ride to the hospital was terrible, very cold and every bump hurt. Looking back I felt like I was a big baby in a lot of ways. I really hadn't read anything and no one taught me about having babies. I had no idea what was going to happen.

Back in the sixties they drugged you a lot, shaved you and gave you killer enemas. They seemed pretty rough with me and I remember crying, screaming and making a fool out of myself because I really thought I was dying. No one talked to me or reassured me that this is normal. I had no understanding of what was going on and don't even remember my doctor's name. I wanted to go home and I decided I never wanted to have another baby.

Finally Todd was born, 6lbs.3oz. He was darling and I fell in love. All my motherly instincts clicked in and I was breast feeding and loving this little baby full time. I felt like my life actually started there. I thought

about someone other than me. I loved being a mom so I started reading anything I could find on mothering, but I could never find anything on birthing. I knew there had to be another way.

After Todd turned two, I was really desiring to have another baby but I wasn't going to do that kind of birth again. It was so humiliating. I went to the library to find a book on birth. I'll never forget the elderly lady at the counter. She was shocked when I asked her for a book on birth. She shushed me and left, came back with a little brown bag and said please don't open this till you get home. The book was *Childbirth Without Fear*, by Grantley Dick Read. I read this book and cried. This was not the birth I went through but the very birth I wanted to experience. I knew I could have it so I started planning to get pregnant.

Its not that easy. It seemed like forever to get pregnant with Joel but the day came. I had read the book a lot and now I had to find a doctor whose name I would remember. I found Dr. K. What a peach. I really liked him. He listened to me and I showed him my book and he said, "I'd like to read that book." I came back a month later and Dr. K. was very excited and said, "I'll help you have the birth you want." I told him I didn't want an episiotomy, no shaving, no enemas, no meds, no needles, no taking my baby away and no pitocin.

The next six months were great as we planned for the birth. I guess that was my first vision, to have an educated, natural birth. At six months I had a bleeding episode and was hospitalized. Dr. K. had to tell me that he thought I would lose the baby. I remember telling him never to say that and I was having this baby and going home. The next morning I left the hospital and Dr. K. was not happy with me. I never looked back.

I was not a Christian yet but I knew God was helping me and I knew He would hold on to my baby. Joel was born, 6lbs.7oz. It was a great birth. I had my dignity and I can say I never let myself have any pain, it was not easy but it was awesome. I had rooming in with baby Joel and Dr. K. said I had the first of everything in this hospital and I believe it changed his practice. I heard years later that he had a very nice practice that was out of the ordinary. I called him when I got out of nursing school. He congratulated me and asked if I would come back and work with him. I was living in Georgia at the time and was flattered but as time moved on I headed for Arkansas instead. I am so glad I did because the vision was for here.

Now about the vision for today. After practicing midwifery for thirty years I realized I had seen some really hard births and I really didn't want to do anymore if birth was going to be so hard. I cried out to the Lord and he told me to go to Habakkuk 2. I read about the vision the Lord instructed him to write and to run with it and surely the Lord would perform it. I asked why? Why did I have to write this now? The Lord said, "It isn't for you. It is for the couples and read Habakkuk 1." So, I read chapter 1 and saw that Habakkuk lived in perilous times, just like us. This word from the Lord is for us today,

"Behold thee among the heathen, and regard, and wonder marvelously: for I will work a work in your days, which ye will not believe, though it be told you." Habakkuk 1:3

It is time to believe the Lord and follow Him closely. The anointing in us and upon us is great for such a time as this. I have been instructing the couples that come to me to write the vision of their baby's birth down and run with it, let God perform it. Since I have done this it has been a joy to go to births again and the outcomes are God ordained. More responsible couples and more peace, more miracles and more joy.

Right, after I got this word from the Lord I shared it at the pregnancy center with a young woman that comes and gets diapers and things for her babies. She was pregnant and said she had high blood pressure and that she had written her vision down.

She told the enemy to get back because high blood pressure was not in her vision and God would keep her. The next day the blood pressure had gone down to normal and she was rejoicing. She said "I love that vision," I said, "It's your vision with the Lord. You and the Lord did that."

Now that some time has passed, so many miraculous and wonderful things have happened from writing the visions down. We have adopted a saying, "If it's not in the vision it can't happen." Thank you Jesus for your provision. Interesting. pro vision!

Oh God you're so good
How can I tell you, thank you?
You're so good
How can I give you, all you've given
How can I give you , all you've given me

Thank you Thank you
You have so many plans for me
Thank you thank you
You have made provision for me
Thank you Thank you
You're So Sweet!

Chapter 2

Fearfully and Wonderfully Made

For thou hast possessed my inward parts; thou hast covered me in my mothers womb. I will praise thee; for I am fearfully and wonderfully made. Marvelous are thy works. and my soul knoweth right well. My substance was not hidden from thee when I was made in secret and intricately wrought in the lowest parts of the earth. Thine eyes did see my substance yet being unformed; and in thy book all my members were written which in continuance were fashioned when as yet there was none of them. How precious also are thy thoughts unto me O God! How great is the sum of them! If I should count them they are more in number than the sand; when I awake I am still with thee. Psalm 139:13-18.

Knowing God's plan for me is important to being able to agree with Him and His word. Knowing He made me fearfully and wonderfully gives me agreement power when fear comes in to exalt itself above the knowledge of God. I can stand fast with the word, nothing is wrong with my baby because God has made this child fearfully and wonderfully. Praising God for the choosing of life and creation he has made is total faith.

It was Tom and Dorothy's birth of Gabriel that tried our faith about Gods plan for his creation. Dorothy's blood was RH negative and she had not gotten a rhogam shot after her first sons birth. [if the mother's blood is negative and the father's blood is positive, a shot is usually recommended for blood incompatibility.

This will help the next baby]. She became worried and felt she was under attack about something being wrong with the baby and possibly loosing the baby after it was born. We prayed together and I admit I had a few thoughts of "what if" myself but we kept going back to God's word. We also talked about repentance of rebellion if it was there. Dorothy did repent and then God gave her a word.

It shall be health to thy navel and marrow to thy bones. Trust in the Lord with all thy heart and lean not unto thine own understanding. In all thy ways acknowledge him and he shall direct thy paths. Be not wise in thine own eyes; fear the Lord, depart from evil. Proverbs 3:5-8.

The problem with rhogam not being given was because of the differences in the blood working against the baby and here was God saying. "Don't worry, trust me, it shall be health to thy navel and marrow to thy bones. The blood will be alright. It is my plan, my creation, I have ordained it, if you believe me and agree with me."

We praised the Lord and rested and Gabriel was born healthy and strong, a perfect child of God. We had a responsibility to God as His people to agree and believe on His word. We did and God's word was established. God is looking for persuaded children, full of faith for everything in our lives. Turning to God for our every thought and deed is total dependence on the One who fearfully and wonderfully made us. Knowing without doubt that God made us perfectly is so important; knowing how much he loves us is monumental. Most of our tragedies and problems are because we don't know how much we are loved. God knows this and is ready to help us at every turn. Turn is the key here, turn to Him, He made us and wants us to come to Him about every little thing. Just like we would our own children, that's how God wants to love us. He says, "Come up here, let Me hold you, let Me swaddle you, let Me bounce you on My knee, I love being with you, having you back on My knee." The Father wants us back. Birth is a wonderful time to come back to Him. We need Him and He needs us, how perfect.

Come back to Me
Don't be afraid, you know My name
Come back to Me

I'm waiting, I'm calling, you to Me
Hurry, hurry, I can't wait to hold you
Come child to Me Come child to Me

Chapter 3

Knowledge of Him

Spending time with the one you love is so wonderful and happiness is automatic. That's how God wants us to view His relationship with us. We are loved and we love. When we are in fear or doubt we need only to seek to visit with the One we love and who loves us, how simple. All I have to do is ask the Holy Spirit to explain anything I need to know about everything, but let me be specific. Just like a child asking questions of adults, we need to hear the specific question in order to answer. Visiting with the Holy Spirit whom Christ sent to comfort, fellowship and teach us is so simple we tend to miss our way. So we must go into the Spirit, pressing in to see God and ask our specific questions of Him. This fellowship takes time and effort.

When there is a battle going on in the mind we are not able to see God. So we get defeated and do not pursue the spirit because it feels foolish to us. When we realize that our reality is in the spirit we will press in and abide with God in the spirit. Such fellowship and blessings are found in a glimpse of God, or to hear His voice, feel His strength, or be filled with peace and joy. Where does this all come from if all this is foolish? It comes from the Spirit. Life in God is real, life changing and energizing. He is the source of life to abide in, the only real life as God planned it, hidden from the lost.

When I first started attending births I would get so confused and mess up a lot. Sometimes I would be really busy with something when I got called and other times didn't feel right about going to a birth. I would go anyway and be there way to early or too late, or they weren't even in labor. I finally asked God to show me what to do? He said, *"I will always give you a peace, no peace no go."* So I started looking for this peace and this is the truth, it works. Sometimes people call me and it sounds urgent, if I don't have a peace about going I don't. Now, some people get offended, but I'll say, "Did it work out?" (and it usually does) "Well then, God was in control, not me."

There are so many distractions and pulls from everywhere today. A person really has to know the voice and peace of God. Even if I miss a birth, God knows I didn't want to, but sometimes He has a better plan than just what I want. Daddies are catching more babies today because God wants them too. We don't like the thought of that but that is God. Daddies are very capable of figuring out what to do. They got into this, they can get a baby out of this, with God's help. I love midwifery but it isn't higher than husband and wife. Marriages need this challenge. We've gotten silly about birth. The picture we have in our heads is not biblical. Fathers can handle helping their wife birth their own baby. Society has ridiculed and moved fathers out of the picture of birth, so midwives should be really eager to put the father back where he belongs, catching his baby and giving the support and love only he can give his wife. This strengthens their marriage and isn't that wonderful, God had that planned. Knowing the Father, God, straightens out everything in your life.

Women today are very strong to the point of annoying. They can boss and manipulate their dear husbands until he just shuts down and can't find a place for himself. He is defined by the woman. I love seeing how my husband does things. He is different from me, and what he does is different. The Father has been showing me that I miss things about Father, God because I'm so busy doing everything my own way. He has a way that will only come through my husband's view of God or their relationship. After all, they are fathers just like the Father. As women we need to trust God to let our husbands handle things and show us this other side. Let him guide you through birth, he has the strength and support to give you. His love will give you a depth a woman can't. I know this is a little touchy but I've really been noticing this where birth is concerned.

Here's an example. I was at a birth of a couple that were both professionals together in business. She went into labor and she only wanted me with her. Her husband was so happy and was trying to give her help and love, but she acted annoyed. She expressed to me that she was so happy I was there and that she felt comfortable with me and could relax. I so wanted to tell her that her husband had a joy that I really didn't have and she needed that right now. It was sad that she had to control everything for herself and not just let it happen. It's like the surprise is taken out and as women, we think we know what we like and that's that.

We as women need to know the Father to really be loved and to love our husbands. They need to be needed and respected, that is just like the Father. When you get to know the Father, He surprises you with outlandish love that will spill over into your relationships and most of all to your husband. It will also spill over into your children. We won't have to control everything they do, we will see the many faces of our Father. Life becomes so crazy in love and fun!

Come on Live Live Live
Let life flow over you
Live Live Live
Drink in the life of God
God has more for you
Live! Life!
Let life be crazy
Live life

Chapter 4

Love

Perfect love casts out fear. There seems to be so much fear in birth. When you know God and His perfect love you can't stay in a place of fear. Truth needs to be examined and to get to the truth you have to go to the Father. His word or His voice needs to be heard to settle the issue of fear. When I hear *"I love you. and will never leave you."* I immediately arrive at a peaceful place even if I still need to deal with the circumstance I am facing. I can do it calmly now and with His help. *"Be still and know that I am God."* sets me in a large place, not in a corner of fear. So what does it mean? What difference does it make? It's the difference between life and death.

Birth is so hidden you can't see the baby that you know is there. That's exactly what is going on in every decision and every action in life. A choice is being made and that choice is going to lead you in a direction of either life or death. You don't always see the results immediately but eventually they tell you where you are going. With birth we want life so the decisions should all be life decisions. Deciding to have a child should be the result of an intimate union with the Lord. Seeking Him for the love, putting a wanting and longing for another child of God here on earth to serve and rejoice with God. When pregnancies are unplanned or rape is involved, God has still clearly said, *"Children are a blessing from the Lord"*, *"Every good and perfect gift comes from above."* Children are blessed. We fall and make mistakes but babies are not mistakes. God's love covers. We always have a way back to the Father, through His Son Jesus, what a beautiful plan.

Know that God's love is to know all His promises. Know you are healed by Jesus' stripes and forgiveness is yours. You have all your needs met according to His riches in Glory. Know that God casts your sin as far as the east is from the west. You have the protection mentioned in psalms 91 and you are abiding in Him. Know that nothing can by any means hurt thee! How do we know God's love?

"Desire the sincere milk of the word that you may grow thereby. That you might be acceptable to God by Jesus Christ. 1 Peter 2:2.

As newborn babies desire the milk of their mothers we are too in order to know that God loves us.

When you grow to know that God accepts you, you will know that God loves you like a son, a child of the Most High God. Everything about life in God is centered around love. It is being loved and loving everyone you encounter.

Just before Christmas, I got a phone call from a family that I had helped the previous January. Mary wanted to tell me the good news that she and Tim were pregnant and would I help them. I squealed! and said "Yes, Yes, when are you due?" She said, "Christmas". I laughed and told Mary that I always go away for Christmas but could get them another midwife as back-up but Mary said, "No, we will wait till you get home. We will trust the Lord. We are not worried, God loves us!" I was a little uncomfortable with this but it is their family and I loved her faith and trust in the Lord.

We left for NY and were there just a few days when Mary called and told me that she was having some labor and what did I think. I told her again that I could get another midwife, but her response was, "Can we just call you when we get in serious labor?" I assured her that would be fine.

About midnight, I crawled into bed up in the attic under the skylight with it snowing and a full moon. It was a gorgeous night. I put my worship music on and curled up. My phone rang and it was Mary and Tim. She was definitely in labor and wanted to put me on speaker phone. We were laughing about all this and asking a lot of questions about how she was doing. She then said, "I am getting in the shower." Both Tim and I laughed, because at the last birth when Mary got in the shower the baby came soon thereafter. Mary also has a tradition she does with a stool on a piece of plastic and a cake pan in front of the stool. She would let the broken water flow into the pan and then the baby would come. I asked Tim, "Are you ready?" He said, "Yes, the pan and stool are in place". We laughed again. The family was also there and you could hear whispers and them praising the Lord. We were all waiting. I thought this could take awhile but then laughed and realized I was in bed and at peace, just enjoy and wait. Soon, Mary came out of the shower and I heard her say, "Tim, have you got the stool and pan ready?" He said, "Yes, all is ready." I asked Mary how she was doing and she said, "God is Good, I am ready." We talked about my new vocation as a phone midwife. We all laughed and I told them all that was missing was me singing and they told me to please sing if I wanted. So I began to sing about the new baby coming into God's love on a snowy night before Christmas. It was a wonderful feeling. I have never felt so blessed. Suddenly I heard a squeal, it was Mary saying, "My water just broke." I said. "Tim did it hit the pan?" Tim said "Yep, perfect shot."

    Mary said it was time to get her to bed. They were excited and I could hear the children whispering that the baby was coming. I sang and thanked Jesus for His perfect way, His perfect love and the banner of love that was over us. Then Mary said, "I have to push." I encouraged her to let it happen and soon I heard baby crying. Tim yelled, "He is here!" I said, "He?" Yes, it was a boy!! I heard Mary talking to the baby comforting him for he was finally here. Then Tim was wanting to know about cutting the cord. I encouraged him to wait till the cord stopped beating and then cut. He got two pieces of shoe string they had sterilized and said, "What do I do with it?" I said, "Just tie in two places and cut between them with the scissors you sterilized." Tim did that and they wrapped baby tight and he started nursing right away.

    Tim then wanted to know about the placenta. I told him it will come, just watch for a little blood and that would be your clue that the placenta is detaching and about to come out. He saw some blood so I told Mary to push if she felt like it and plop, out came the placenta all in one piece. There was hardly any bleeding after that. She was nursing baby, feeling great and I could hear her talking to the children, showing them their new baby brother.

All is well, God loves us, and we are a loved people. In the bible is a reference to the Key of David. I always wondered what that was. I believe it is where David says, "God is mine and I am His." What would our world be like if we really thought and lived like that is the plan of the Lord. *You are mine and I am yours.* Yes, perfect birth, perfect surrender, perfect love.

> A snowy night, you're light
> A snowy night, so right
> Everything feels so good
> Happiness in the night
> Secrets of angels carrying light
> What just happened ?
> Was so right
> Baby coming in the light
> Baby wrapped in pure, white light
> Families full of lights
> On a snowy white night
> Oh, my God, you are so right
> Thank you, for showing me, the light!

Chapter 5

Faith

Faith is my job. God's job is the author and finisher of my faith. God tells us, "*Without faith it is impossible to please God and the Just shall live by Faith.*" God has told me I am to believe I have faith because He gave it to me and then I am to use it. Do not worry about the outcome for that is His job. Mine is to release my faith and stand, never being moved so that God can take the faith and finish the work. This has become very simple to me and seems to be a very good way to explain our agreement and co-working with Christ.

When Christ comes He wants to find faith on the earth. This must be very important then and it is our job to be in faith at all times. God said He would make us able to do His will so He has equipped us. He has given us everything that pertains to life and godliness. I am positioning myself to turn to God for everything and to repent when I do things of my own knowledge and don't trust God with it. I need to give to the Lord everything I have gathered as knowledge and then only give out as my knowledge of the Lord says. Jesus said. "*I only do what I see my Father doing.*"

Jesus was learned and intelligent, after all He was the son of God. So why did He only do what His father did? Because He would be in total agreement with God and there is power in that. Obedience is a part of that as well as unity of the spirit. I need to walk in spirit and in truth. I can only get this with seeking the knowledge of God. *Seek ye first the Kingdom of God and all these things will be added unto you.* I believe if I didn't use my knowledge but sought to use God's knowledge in every circumstance I would see miracles, gifts of faith, words of knowledge, gifts of healing, tongues, interpretation, and deliverance. Reading the word of God and then applying it to the situation is the answer for every need and every person, no exception. The Lord gave me a dream one night. I was asking how to see prayer answered and He said:

"Take the word and give it to me in faith knowing that I will do it and I will come and take the words and fly away and create that which you have given me. Don't ever take it back just stand and watch Me."

This brings to mind, "Watch and pray."

Stand fast in the faith in one spirit. stand and don't be moved with all stand and stand again. Mark 14:38.

We are suppose to stand and wait and watch, believing. It helps to know God's word accomplishes what it is sent to do and does not return void. Thank God He is the maker of heaven and earth. We can have confidence in His continuing to create out of nothing.

"Through faith we understand that the worlds were framed by the word of God." Hebrews 11:3

Faith is giving to God and waiting on God, never moving. Set your feet on the rock and keep a word of faith in your mouth. Ask the Holy Spirit to help keep a watch over your speech and strengthen you to stand in the face of doubt and fear and not to move. Set your face as flint and do not move to the right or the left but look ahead for God will create it from His word.

"Faith is the substance of things hoped for the evidence of things unseen. Through faith we understand that the worlds were framed by the word of God so that things which are seen were not made of things which do appear." Hebrews 11:1-3

"Let us come boldly unto the throne of grace that we may obtain *mercy. and find grace to help in time of need." Hebrews 4:16.*

We have a blood covenant with God through Christ Jesus. This means that everything that is God's is mine and everything that is mine is God's. We have inherited everything that Jesus did for us at Calvary. We have been redeemed from the curse of sin, poverty and sickness. When we go into God and ask for help we will receive the love and blessings of God. Every promise is ours. We receive our answer in the spirit. Jesus is our answer. Everything He did on the cross is ours.

Picture God on His throne and believe that we are obtaining mercy from Him and receiving our answer. He gives us everything that pertains to life and godliness. God says;

"Take your evidence, your answer, and go back to earth and hold on to your evidence. It has now become substance. You have received it in the spirit and you now must show that you have evidence in the natural. This evidence is your faith."

My faith is my evidence. I had faith that I received my answer before God. He's my witness. It is done. Now I rejoice that I have received my answer and have the faith to prove it. So it is done. Now everyone I see says; "Where is it"? I say; "Right here, it's my faith, I saw my Father give it to me. He's promised me and now it is done. I have all His riches, healing, peace, love, forgiveness, deliverance, and all His character and possessions."

When your faith has taken a giant step forward is when the enemy comes in. It can be in the form of your own mind, other people or just an intensifying of the problem. STOP it in its tracks immediately! You know God's word. Take a swing at the voices and the opposition with the word of God. Take the word God gives you or one that is applicable to the situation and remember:

"God has given you everything that pertains to life and godliness." 2 Peter 1:3

"Satan came to kill, steal and destroy but Jesus came to bring Life and Life abundantly." John 10:10

Protect the anointing of Jesus Christ in you and hold on to your faith. Take the whole armor of God.

"That ye may be able to stand against the wiles of the devil."
Ephesians 6:11-20.

Chapter 6

Faith Like This I Have Not Seen

I have not found such great faith Math 8:10

There was a centurion that came to Jesus and pleaded with Him to heal his servant that was paralyzed and tormented. Jesus said "I will come and heal him." The centurion said, "Lord, I am not worthy that you should come under my roof. But only speak a word and my servant will be healed. For I also am a man under authority, having soldiers under me. And I say to this one, 'Go' and he goes and to another 'Come' and he comes and to my servant 'Do this and he does it'." When Jesus heard it, He marveled and said to those who followed. "Assuredly, I say to you, I have not found such great faith, not even in Israel."

I have seen all kinds of faith stories but this one is awesome. It is about a couple who have had tragedies and heart aches in their lives. The loss of twins at birth and a long 14 year wait to get pregnant again. She finally got pregnant, had a little girl and while nursing noticed a lump in her breast. She developed mastitis and her breast began to deteriorate. She continually cried out to the Lord for healing. She then got pregnant again and came to see me. We had such a wonderful visit and I kept seeing this clear sparkling look in both her and her husband's eyes. I knew they were suffering but I saw such great faith. They knew her breast was in really bad shape and she had other symptoms but they kept asking the Lord what should they do. *"Trust me"* and *"Don't be afraid"* were the answers they received.

I had fears too but seeing their great faith in the face of such suffering, I had to have the fear of God on me to up-hold them and pray for them. God was in control and He had a plan for them. Even though it appeared the enemy had the control I knew they knew God was the Victor.

Months went by with lots of praying, reading the word, declaring, fasting, and crying out. She seemed to get worse. One of her eyes became blind and she had terrible pain and bleeding of her breast. Then she had nausea and vomiting but her baby was so active and kept growing. As the months progressed she appeared to be getting worse. She moved into her mother and father's house so they could get help. She had many moments of difficult breathing, bleeding, pain and fear but in it all she still had wonderful times with Jesus. She had wonderful visions and miraculous times of Jesus taking the pain and the fear away. She often said "Even in all of this trial I wouldn't have wanted to miss this time with Jesus." She was committed to trusting the Lord's healing power.

A month before she was going to give birth I had every desire to be with her and help her but I had no release in the spirit to be there. I told her I didn't know if I would be there and would know when I needed to. I tried to figure out if I was in fear or unbelief. But I just felt I was obeying to stay put and listen for the Spirit. I had a sense that her faith was going to be activated by the birth and I should not be in the way. A week after she asked me if I would be there she went into labor and she did not call me. Her sister-in-laws helped her and they called me to tell me the incredible story.

She had labored hard at first and then stopped. They got discouraged about it but the next day she started laboring again and then stopped again. They called me at some point to ask for counsel about the labor starting and stopping. I told her sister-in-law that this was the Lord to labor her slowly and easy so she had energy to birth. The third day of labor she called her sister-in-laws and they came. She was complete and a bulging bag of waters. They told her she could push but she just didn't have the strength. Her water broke and a cord came out, about 8" of it. The sister-in-law felt the cord and it wasn't beating. She said she never had any fear, she just knew the mommy had to push. She told her to push and she couldn't so they pushed down and out on her tummy and the baby plopped out. He squeaked a little, then they suctioned him and he was fine. He cried, pinked up and they put him to the breast and he nursed. He was named Caleb and weighed a little over 5 pounds. Praise the Lord!

Caleb in the bible was the servant of the Lord that went in with Joshua to spy out the promise land and had come back with a good report.So she is nursing the good report and promises. What a miracle and what Miracles are yet to come. Her healing has not manifested fully, but she has successfully nursed her baby. He is fat and happy. She and her husband continue to hold on to Jesus and they amaze me with their faith and love. Praise God !! Continue in prayer daily for them. God is Good!!

Faith is the substance of things hoped for, the evidence of things unseen. Hebrews 11:1

But without faith it is impossible to please Him, for he who comes to God must believe that He is and that He rewards those who diligently seek him. Hebrews 11:6

The couple is still standing today, ever aware of the presence of the Father's love and care. Growing closer to God then anyone could possibly imagine, they are an encouragement of trust and love. I pray victory for their family! God Bless this family!

I stand in the river
Everything lives in the river
Everyone come to the river
And live!

Chapter 7

Living in the Promises

God's promises are established and to live and move in them is to walk upright and in the will of God. Surround yourself with the word of God and speak the word and meditate on the word. Sing the word and eventually you will become convinced that the word is established and you will be planted in God and His word. Perfect agreement with God will be established and you will be trusting totally in Him. There will be no way to be moved. The word is His promise. We are sons and inheritors of His promise. We have to know in our hearts what we have inherited in order to have it. Find out what you have and then speak it out, sing it out, pray it and command it to be because it is the way of God. Thank God for His word. It is life to us who have been crucified in Christ.

Here is a collection of promises from Scripture that you can hang on to and believe God for.

Luke 18:8
"I tell you, he will see that they get justice and quickly, However, when the Son of Man comes, will he find faith on the earth?"

Hebrews 10:38
"But my righteous one will live by faith. And if he shrinks back I will not be pleased with him."

Galatians 3:11
"Clearly no one is justified before God by the law because The righteous will live by faith."

Isaiah 61:1-3 (KJV)
"The Spirit of the Lord God is upon me, because the Lord hath anointed me to preach good tidings unto the meek; he hath sent me to bind up the brokenhearted, to proclaim liberty to the captives, and the opening of the prison to them that are bound; To proclaim the acceptable year of the Lord and the day of vengeance of our God; to comfort all that mourn; To appoint unto them that mourn in Zion, to give unto them beauty for ashes, the oil of joy for mourning, the garment of praise for the spirit of heaviness; that they might be called trees of righteousness, the planting of the Lord, that he might be glorified.

Psalms 119 (KJV)
I will delight myself in thy statutes: I will not forget thy word. Deal bountifully with thy servant that I may live and keep thy word. My soul melteth for heaviness: strengthen thou me according unto thy word. For ever O Lord thy word is settled in heaven. Thy faithfulness is unto all generations: thou hast established the earth and it abideth. Thou art my hiding place and my shield: I hope in thy word. Depart from me ye evildoers: for I will keep the commandments of my God. Uphold me according unto thy word that I may live: and let me not be ashamed of my hope.

Psalm 130:5
I wait for the Lord my soul doth wait and in his word do I hope.

Galatians 2:20
I am crucified with Christ: nevertheless I live; yet not I but Christ liveth in me: and the life which I now live in the flesh I live by the faith of the Son of God who loved me, and gave himself for me.

Hebrews 4:1
Let us therefore fear, lest, a promise being left us of entering into his rest, any of you should seem to come short of it.

Hebrews 6:15
And so, after he had patiently endured, he obtained the promise.

A young mother came to me after hearing that a friend of hers had a homebirth. After I met with her and her husband I realized they had no idea what wonderful promises they were going to find. It's like knowing someone is going to find a treasure chest but you just have to lead them to it because they would never find it quickly. We were going along fine but

I hadn't seen the father a lot and that kind of concerned me. Nevertheless, I was developing a strong foundation of trust with the mother. She missed a visit and next thing I knew she was dealing with a breech baby and went to see a doctor.

The report from the doctor was that her baby would die and she could never have a child as large as hers and that her pelvis was inadequate. I was shocked when she tearfully announced all this news. I said, "What do you think about this report?" She said. "I don't believe any of it. That's why I wanted a homebirth." Thank goodness she was trusting in God and His creation.

"We are fearfully and wonderfully made." Psalms 139:14

I checked her and really felt that baby was head down so I asked if she would go to another doctor that I knew who would be more trusting of home birth and she agreed. She saw the doctor and he reported that the baby's head was down and that she had a very adequate pelvis. "Praise the Lord"! So we got ready for a homebirth.

Soon after, she went into some labor symptoms and I got a frantic call late one evening from her in-laws. They said she had been having contractions all day and had been crying. They were full of fear and told me that they were concerned something was wrong and the doctor had said she couldn't have this baby and what if it died. What was I going to do?

My alarm went off and I began to tell them of the promises Jesus Christ has given us if we will only believe. I knew I was telling them things they didn't believe or understand but it was time for shutting up the enemy. The couple didn't have a phone so I had to ask the mother in-law to have her call me. After talking with the mommy I realized the parents were believing a curse the doctor had put on this couples birth. I prayed God would make a way to show His never failing love and promises to the believer.

My mother and I went to visit them a week later. I was hoping to get to talk with the expectant mother and father alone. We went into the house and I realized I had left my bag in the car and discovered I had locked the keys in the car. I had never done this before and I had no idea how to unlock the doors. We had to go up to the in-laws house to use the phone. I called my husband and he hadn't a clue so I asked the expectant daddy if he had any suggestions so he came back to his house with me to help unlock the car. When my mother and I had started out early that morning I realized a window in the back was down just a little and was going to roll it up but a little voice told me not to. Well, thank God, because the daddy was able to put a plastic pipe in and flip a switch to open the doors. I thought how odd, because now the couple was alone with me without the in-laws present. We could talk and pray.

I checked the mother out and found she was dilated to 2cm. and the babies head was down and 70 % effaced. This was a good report. We all got excited and I could hear the bad report looming but God was more powerful in me and I just let the excitement flow. I prophesied a fast easy birth with a very lively mom and baby like the Hebrew women and that I would make it back for the birth. I began to tell the couple how important it was to bind up the lying curse that the doctor reported according to Matthew 18:18. I asked the couple to speak to their parents concerning the choice of standing in faith with us or not being a part of the birth. How important it was to have faith and not doubt at the birth and that hindering spirits must be bound. They both agreed to talk to their parents and friends to stand in faith or not come around.

Mom and I left and had a wonderful trip home. Now I was excited for the birth and looking forward not fearful. A week later I was getting dressed for work when I got a call from the daddy early in the morning. He said, "She's ready, having 2 minute contractions." I figured this could take a while since it was her first baby and to start at 2 minutes was usually a sign of early inadequate contractions. I felt to go since it was a distance to drive and she might need help to get going. I hopped in the car and immediately the Lord was telling me to stand and not be moved. This would be a joyous birth and a Glory to God. I shouted every promise I could think of and sang victory songs.

When I arrived I saw she was very calm and seemingly not in much labor so I decided to check her and see how she was doing. She was 7cm dilated and a bulging bag of waters. The baby's heart beat was good. The Lord was telling me to just sit back and not to check her any more and just let Him deliver this baby. I wanted to break the water so I could see if it was clear or not. I could hear in the back of my head "a dead baby and she can't have this size a baby." God said: *"Bind that voice and trust me. This is my birth and you will see the Glory I have in my promises."* So I relaxed. I visited with daddy and talked of the Lord and gave comfort to the momma. I truly enjoyed myself and felt they were having a joyful time.

I asked where their parents were and they didn't know. They had left in the truck but hadn't arrived back yet which was kind of unusual but we knew God was in control. A dear friend came just as momma was pushing and she helped. The water broke and it was thick green. Not usually a good sign but instead of fear I laughed and said:

"Count it all joy when you fall into various trials and tribulations for it works patience. But let patience have her perfect work, that ye may be perfect and entire wanting nothing." James 1:4

God spoke to me that His voice was the voice of love and who could love me and this precious couple more? He or the doctor? I laughed and said, "You Lord. You Love me more than any man. I love you Lord for your faithfulness endures for ever." I confessed clear lungs for baby and a perfect birth and a healthy and lively momma. Praise God! That baby came out screaming and pink not at all compromised. The waters that broke were green to start with but the last of it was as clear as water. Praise God! It was a perfectly wonderful birth and Satan was totally defeated.

"And the sheep follow Him, for they know His voice. And a stranger they will not follow but will flee from Him, for they know not the voice of strangers." John 10:4

"Christ has by His Divine power given us everything that pertains to life and godliness through Christ Jesus." 2 Peter 2:3

Isn't it better to follow the Good Shepherd than man? Thank you Father your word is better than Life. It is Life.

Chapter 8

Father, Mother and Child

Fathers taking authority over their family is important in seeing God work. Families need to be taught how God honors with power those that walk in agreement with His word. I have seen couples that need a miracle of faith, and need to stand believing. When the father takes the leadership in the family and they stand in agreement on a word from God there is power and prayer is answered.

A family I had helped moved away and called me when they were pregnant with another child. They had a midwife but just found out they had a breech baby and were upset. I asked to talk to the daddy and I told him that he needed to take authority over his child and command the baby to turn and get head down in Jesus name. We encouraged each other in the Lord and testified of His power in us and how wonderfully God had worked in the other children's births. The baby did turn and we rejoiced. We hung up and I gave it all to the Lord and I didn't think about it again. They called and asked me to fly to Scotland to help them. I laughed and said, "I don't think I can, I'm too busy and can't get away, sorry." Then the father asked would I pray about it so of course I said, I would.

So about a week later I felt I should honor the father's wishes and pray about going to Scotland. So I prayed and to my surprise the Lord said, "You are going." I said, "Rick can't go and I don't want to be by myself." The Lord said, "I will be with you, I really want you to go, we will have fun." So, off to Scotland I went, I was to be there 10 days. On the 5_{th} day, baby Grace came so beautifully in the night, in the birth tub. What a great time we all had and it was beautiful there, right on the ocean. The time of year was January, so it was very cold but what an experience. Such a lovely, Godly family and great adventure.

On the way home the airplane was very empty and I felt like I was by myself, the Lord said, "Come away with me." We had a blast on that lane. The Father talked to me about my family, my life in Him, His plans for me, how to trust Him and believe His word. I covered my head with a blanket and I cried and laughed and talked to Jesus all the way home. It was a powerful time in my life. He thanked me for my obedience and I thanked Him for His faithfulness to turn the baby and then for bringing baby while I was there. I thanked Him for His love toward all of us and for escorting me to Scotland.

At home now on my birthday I was praying and I asked Jesus to let me encourage someone today that was really needing it. It was 7 o'clock in the morning when the phone rang. It was a woman that I had never delivered but with her last two children she called me for prayer and encouragement each time and had wonderful births. She was pregnant again, overdue and needed some help overcoming fear. I got so excited and the anointing came to share some real insight into how perfect love casts out fear and how when the baby is coming so many women get overwhelmed and loose their joy or peace.

The Holy Spirit said

"Have them put their hand on the baby's head. It will assure them and give love to both baby and mother so that fear will be overcome by love."

It seems like such a little thing but doing this will perfect a birth. The mother was very excited now to deliver and was not at all fearful. It always amazes me to see how perfectly in order everything God has made and set up. I assisted a very young couple that didn't know the Lord and were very unhappy with their lives. I felt they had no where to turn so they were forced to be placed with me. I immediately took advantage of this situation and the anointing of God took over. I honestly can't say I knew what I was doing but I've learned to follow the Holy Spirit and end up in a very wonderful place. I started out by praying with her even though I couldn't see that she was really with me. Actually she was shocked at me and just listening.

Then the birth came and I had prayed that the daddy would be there and the family would not interfere. He was there and the family went shopping for baby things. It was the middle of the night. Her water had broke and contractions were very light. I checked her and she was just 3cm. and 50% effaced so I thought we may have some time. I gave her some labor tincture and tucked her and her husband in for the duration. They seemed so young and vulnerable. He seemed attentive to her and I could feel love but also the pull from the world. I saw so clearly how the world pushes us away from the goodness and happiness God has for us.

This birth situation was so foreign to them that they needed each other. I had not met daddy before this but I looked directly into his eyes and he liked me and was intrigued by all this and a little afraid. I laid down and maybe an hour went by when he came to tell me she needed me. Her contractions were close and lots of bloody show and a little push was starting to come. I checked her and she was complete so we started to work into pushing. She said it felt better to push and actually rested to the point of sleep between contractions.

I was happy for them and praising the Lord. Daddy was stroking her face and holding her hand. He never took his eyes off her. They both felt this was a little girl and had no boy names. I asked them if they wanted their parents there and they did so I prayed they'd make it and they did. God is good! Just as baby was coming out I had the mother put her hand on the babies head and she squealed for joy. Daddy looked then and got so excited. Her mother was crying tears of joy and helping me with wet warm cloths for her bottom while daddy was blowing very vigorously with the mom to keep her from tearing. This is when someone gets in the mothers face and blows like they are blowing a candle flame out. Out came baby Kenzie, 6lbs 12 oz. She was beautiful and I could see daddy fell in love with her. We oogled and praised God, laughed a lot and mother was so at peace. Her husband hugged her and described the baby to her. He said, "She looks just like you honey, she's beautiful."

I sat back and just watched it all. God moving when there were no counselors or formulas to save them, only God. Only God can save and deliver. Only God can restore love and give a secure, happy future. Daddy cut the cord. He never wavered as he cut with authority. I quietly prayed he'd never forget that he was operating in the peace, love, confidence and acceptance of the Lord. Now acceptance, this is where God was way ahead of anything I could ask or think. God is so good!

Everybody went to bed because it was early morning and too quiet to stay up. I lay down but couldn't sleep. I just laid and listened for activity in their room not really aware I was doing that. I asked the Holy Spirit to tell me if they needed anything. I was so happy and content for everything and everybody I guess I was overwhelmed with thankfulness.

About 4'oclock. I heard baby crying as I had a few times since she was born. I listened but then felt I had to go in to see. It was weird because what happened next was not me but the spirit in me. I opened their door and the three of them were laying in the bed. Daddy was trying to get baby to nurse and mother was so tired and frustrated. I could see what was happening. I walked over and looked daddy in the eye. I took my finger and just flipped her nipple in the baby's mouth. She got hold and just sucked away. I turned their light off and went to bed.

The next morning I got up and went in. Mother was in the bathtub and daddy was sitting there looking at the baby. Daddy and my eyes met and we smiled. A lot had happened between all of us and I can honestly say I loved him and his family. I asked, "How did you sleep? He said, "Great after you got the baby to nurse. She nursed all night." Then mother came out and she looked great. She was combing her long brown hair and she had a big smile. I prayed that smile would last forever. It can, I know. But will it? God has keeping power over us! Keep us Lord! She proceeded to tell me how great she slept after I helped put the baby on the breast. The thought just popped into my mind that she was not going to breastfeed the baby and I realized what had taken place last night.

God had anointed me with a clarity of what had happened with the nursing and what it means to all of us that believe. To believe and walk in faith we must nurse on our Father's word to grow. We need help to nurse, to stay in the word of God. The world does not understand the Kingdom of God. This is a Kingdom life, we have to learn of it and the only way to learn of the Kingdom is from the Father, Son, and Holy Spirit. How they teach is through relationship. A baby nurses and it is the beginning of their relationship out of the womb.

I finally got home and Rick gave me a much needed massage. He was massaging my legs and hips very deeply. When he laid his hands on my stomach and prayed over me I felt totally at peace and a song came up out of my belly. A song we had sung in our band when we were first Christians. It's in 1 Peter 2:2.

As new born babes, desire the sincere milk of the word that ye may grow by it. If so be ye have tasted that the Lord is gracious; to whom, coming as unto a living stone. disallowed indeed of men but chosen of God, and precious. Ye also as living stone, are built up a spiritual house, an holy priesthood, to offer up spiritual sacrifice, acceptable to God by Jesus Christ.

Acceptable to God by Jesus Christ, that's what we can be if we nurse on the pure milk of the word. That little baby needed to be accepted by her mother and father. She needed to know it by her mother nursing her. It wasn't about food; a bottle could have been given. It was about us learning that God had set up for us to nurse on the pure milk of the word and through that we would find acceptance. This little baby needed to nurse on her mother's breast for warmth and acceptance. Acceptance carries with it security, love, trust, kindness, joy, meekness, longsuffering, patience, peace, and faith. These are the fruit of the spirit.

I've noticed that mother's having difficulty in their position in the family often do not want to breast feed and have no desire or supposed ability to nurse their babies. They make excuses and usually find reasons to stop or they are forced to. These moms need acceptance from God by Jesus Christ too. Just think, a key to humanity feeling secure and loved is right under our nose, right in our chest and leads us to the scripture:

As newborn babes, desire the sincere milk of the word, that ye may grow thereby. 1 Peter 2:2

How will we grow up and be accepted by God, but by the word of God showing us the love of God and what Jesus did for us. He made us acceptable to God. Feed upon the word. Nurse at the Many-Breasted-One, Jehovah-Jireh. He will supply all our needs according to His riches in glory through Christ Jesus. We lack for nothing. He has met all our needs. Doesn't that make you feel accepted?

Chapter 9

Waiting

Something I have consistently noticed about pregnancy is waiting. There are times when patience is very present and seems to be totally God given. Then there are times when I can not understand where patience and faith went but instead anxiousness comes in and destroys the peace and joy for a couple. I cannot reason with them and only through prayer and the word of God can we get back to a place of peace.

Getting to this peace is necessary because fear and stress begin to undermine and wear on their confidence in themselves. Most importantly God is not allowed to rule and reign in this place of fear and anxiety.

Casting down imaginations and every high thing that exalts its self above the knowledge of God, and bringing into captivity every thought to the obedience of Christ; And having a readiness to punish all disobedience when your obedience is fulfilled. Do you look on things after the outward appearance? If any man trust to himself that he is Christ's, let him of himself think this again, that as he is Christ's, even so are we Christ's. 2 Corinthians 10:5-7

Count it all joy when you fall into various trials knowing this, that the testing of your faith worketh patience. James1: 2-3.

Usually right at the end of a pregnancy a sense of reality comes in and a war starts between reason and faith. The key here is that you need your reason to exercise your faith. God's word is truth so you need a lot of God's word to flood you when your mind starts telling you something is going to go wrong or that no one can have anything perfect here on earth. This is when the devil moves in with erosion giving you the thought's of the world. Blast it away with the living word of God. Go to the Lord and humble yourself before Him and give up all your thoughts and submit to the knowledge of Him, His voice. Hear what the word of the Lord would say to you. This will begin the victory over every situation.

Be of good cheer for I have overcome the world. John 16:33

For whatever is born of God overcometh the world: and this is the victory that overcometh the world, even our faith. 1 John 5:4

Kick out every thought that does not line up with God's word. Peace will fill you up and joy will fill your heart. Don't let go of what you know to be true for this is faith holding fast to the confession of faith. Standing in faith and not being moved into fear is obedience to God and there is no other way. Being moved by feelings and fears is sin that undermines our walk of faith and all of God's work in us. Sometimes I feel like pregnancy is a great time of trial. Holding on to all we know to be true is a great victory. The baby is the fruit of life in us in Christ.

Waiting for a baby to arrive is a true faith walk. There is little you can do to bring on contractions that cause the dilating of the cervix. By trying to hurry things you will cause strong Braxton-Hicks contractions which is false labor. It is better to rest in His hands and trust for timing and a perfect way. "A wise woman builds her house. A foolish woman tears down with her hands." I've often told women they can use castor oil to start their contractions if a woman is over due and the cervix is ready. This does usually start things either immediately or with in a few days. Nipple stimulation is very helpful and having a friend's baby nurse from you will often start labor. A lot of love making will often cause contractions. Letting the sperm lie in the womb all night will break down the cervix and soften enough that labor may begin.

Rest instead of striving is always the key to labor. When in doubt, rest and rest again. Or stand and stand again in faith patiently trusting in God. Surrender to Gods voice and His spirit,

His plan not yours. Knowing that God knows no restraint or restriction to save or deliver. This is like salvation. You may pray in faith for someone to get saved then you must not let go of that faith asking God to increase your faith to stand and not waiver. Wait and do not dig your seed of faith up. If you dig it up and plant it over and over again you will never see the full ear of corn. Hold fast to the knowledge of your faith. God never lets us down if we have believed from our heart and not doubted. We have it backwards when we take birth so lightly in a spiritual sense and then in the physical we are so heavy with the burden of it. We should instead take this life very seriously in the spirit even before conception. This is where the true walk of faith begins. Then we carry on going from step to step, glory to glory giving God the praise and resting in His love. Striving is trying to bring on labor and pushing to have the baby when the world floods in with fears. "I'm overdue. I'm getting to big. Baby will be too big. I'm having too many contractions with no progress, what's wrong"? GO TO GOD!!! Fall in His loving arms.

"Perfect love casts out fear." Strive not in the flesh but strive to enter into the rest. Let us labor therefore to enter into that rest lest any man fall after the same example of unbelief. For the word of God is living and powerful and sharper than any two-edged sword piercing even to the dividing asunder of soul and spirit, and of the joints and marrow and is a discerner of the thoughts and intents of the heart." Hebrews 4:11.

We can know that faith and rest will change the situation. I've seen many couples going off into fear and striving but when God is brought into first place the two-edged sword of the word pierces the fear and rightly divides between the truth and lies and you can see the situation get under control of the spirit. The reality is that it is the Spirit of the Living God that makes the difference. There is nothing the flesh can do but accept wrong thinking and lies. Many births and problems are changed instantly by obeying God and not striving. REST!

My son was getting married in May so I arranged for all babies due around the end of May to be prepared to find other midwives or pray believing that God would make a way for them and to be at peace with me leaving. Well, what a test of faith for all involved. I had two babies overdue and three babies not due for several weeks deciding they were going to go before I left. It seemed they thought that just deciding they wanted to have the baby was how it worked. I learned a lot about faith versus desire. Watching these couples will and desire these babies to come at a particular time was not faith. How we got to faith took prayer and the word of God firmly and strongly applied.

Lea and Michael were having their first child. Lea had such a strong sense of what she wanted, a totally natural, God given birth. They did their birth vision and we were prayed up and ready. I didn't sense any fear from either of them. Three days overdue Lea called and her water had broken. They were so excited. I made arrangements for them to keep me posted of baby moving, good and clear waters and of course any contractions. Well, 12 hours went by and they were doing ok, so then we tried some enemas and walking. They were still excited when 24 hours went by and baby was still not coming.

I decided then to go over and listen to baby and see if I couldn't get some contractions going. Of course, we were praying and calling out to God, it was time, bring a baby. I got to their house and I could see Lea and Michael were getting a little worried, mostly because they had made the mistake of notifying people that the water had broke. So they were getting responses like, "I can have the EMS there in 5 minutes." Wow, we had to shut the phone calls down so we could continue to stand in faith.

The hard part about waiting in today's world is communications. Everybody knows our business and then you get all the imaginations and interference. So we talked and prayed and rested. It was a pretty April day so I did some paper work, read my bible a lot and visited with Lea and Michael. It was truly restful and enjoyable. Once I made the decision I was here, I relaxed and it was truly a joy to be with them waiting for God to show up, in birth. I learned a lot about them and we all got really close. I slept a lot and needed it for what was to come, I wanted this baby to come almost as much as they did.

We were watching television for awhile and laughing at the show we were watching. We were trying some new acupuncture on her arm and feet as well as castor oil on her belly. All these things helped but it still seemed like this baby would never come. Lea was also taking lots of water, Echinacea, vitamin c, calcium, & labor tincture. I had not checked her because I wanted to keep her infection free, this was the main concern. Suddenly she had a contraction then another and within an hour we were in full blown labor. Her mom came and it was so nice to have help and get to know her as well. Soon we were in hard labor, no turning back. Baby was good, momma was good, now, let's see this baby. Michael was so attentive to Lea it was wonderful. She went through the night and into the morning when finally little Landry was born, beautiful and prefect. Michael made French toast, I knew he must have been really tired but he was wonderful and it was so neat to see Lea in the recliner with baby. What a beautiful 40 hour wait. Lea has told me, she is really looking forward to her next birth because she loved her labor time and yes even the wait. She said 'I can't wait to get pregnant and have another baby." I heard later that they are pregnant again! Praise you Lord!!

Waiting for you Lord
What can we do?
Waiting for you Lord
Watching with you
Knowing your perfect
Your plan is good
Waiting and watching
We worship you
Trusting and praying
We wait for you
Knowing it's good
We wait with you
Come let us see
And hold you
We will never be waiting without you!
You are waiting too!

Chapter 10

Priorities

Let us hear the conclusion of the whole matter: Fear God and keep His commandments; for this is the whole duty of man.
Ecclesiastes 12:13

Looking to God for everything in our life should be what we've learned to do as Christians. But somehow when it comes to conception or birth we turn to the world for the way to walk. I cannot believe this is our whole duty. God is our Creator. He wants to be a part of our lives. Leaving Him out of the planning and conception of our families is something to fear. God has the perfect way for us and He does not want us to just follow what everyone else is doing but be a peculiar people that He is talking to and guiding. Putting God first will set everything you do in order. Being out of the will of God and not letting Him guide your steps will bring error and problems.

"We have not because we ask not." "Ye ask and receive not because ye ask amiss that you receive it upon your own lusts. Whosoever, therefore will be a friend of the world is the enemy of God." James 3:1-4

I was in a Christian book store one day when a mother and daughter walked up to me to say hi. I hadn't seen them in a long time and they began to tell me how the daughter had just got back from the doctors office. I asked what was wrong and they told me Dana had wanted to get pregnant and was newly married. She and her husband were desiring a baby but the doctor told them, "You have a condition called endometriosis and you can't conceive or carry a baby let alone deliver one." I could see that Dana had totally accepted this report. I asked "What do you think God would say about this?" Dana said, "God would want me to have a baby." Yes!!! I got excited and asked if I could pray for her and her baby. I knew a baby was on its way. We all got excited. The prayer was totally God. I could feel God's love for their family and His excitement over new found hope and faith.

We prayed the blessings of God over her family, her womb, and the new baby soon to be conceived. We bound the devil from bad reports and trying to curse her womb because what God has blessed cannot be cursed. We began to rejoice right there in the book store. None of us cared about what people thought. Dana and her husband were going to have a family, yes! God is Good! I left hugging and kissing them. What a joy to see hope and to be kicking despair and loss out the door, with the bad report. Let's speak and choose life. God commands us:

"The power of life and death are in the tongue" Proverbs 18:21

"I call heaven and earth to record this day against you, that I have set before you life and death, blessing & cursing: therefore choose life, that thou and thy seed may live." Deut. 30:19

As I left I had the thought 'you just gave someone hope for something that may not happen, that is not love.' The Lord stepped in and said,

"I Am the one who gives life, no one else. Trust My words and My ways, they are perfect, always give hope, that is choosing life. That is Love, My Love!

I immediately relaxed and felt happy for Dana, knowing I'd hear soon they were pregnant. About several months later Dana's mother called to tell me the good news that Dana and Jeff are pregnant. They said they are so happy and thanked me for truth and prayers. Later that day I heard the Lord say, "Thank you for your obedience." I was already singing songs of deliverance:

My ways are not your ways
My voice will give sound to the way

Follow me and you will see
Follow my word and you will see
How much I love and care for thee
Follow me Follow me
I have so much for you to see
Follow my word and you will see
More blessing then man can see.

Chapter 11

Anointing

The Spirit of the Lord God is upon me because the Lord hath anointed me to preach good tidings unto the meek. He hath sent me to bind up the brokenhearted, to proclaim liberty to the captives, and the opening of the prison to those who are bound, to proclaim the acceptable year of the Lord and the day of vengeance of our God. To comfort all that mourn, to appoint unto those who mourn in Zion, to give unto them beauty for ashes, the oil of joy for mourning, the garment of praise for the spirit of heaviness that they might be called trees of righteousness, the planting of the Lord, that he might be glorified. Isaiah 61:1-3

From the beginning of my walk with God He has impressed me with this scripture. He has spoken it to me, asked me to turn to it, sang it to me and revealed it in intercessory prayer. In my dreams He has shown me the anointing and how it breaks the yoke (things I am in bondage to) in my life as well as in others. I've become stronger in weakness with this word. Knowing that the Spirit of the Lord has anointed me, you and in fact all believers, gives us hope to face the impossible. It gives us the joy to meet the day, the authority to change our circumstances and the love that covers and casts out fear. In prayer and fellowship with the Lord is where the anointing soaks in and changes us. We can know this scripture and know that it is true. Only through worship, prayer and fellowship with God do we begin to see the character of God. We experience Him, His love, His word, His care, authority, power, peace, faith, and confidence.

Recently after a birth, Rick and I went out on the lake

where we have our boat and abided in the peace of God. We sat for a long time looking at the stars, watching the wind, clouds, water, and hearing only the sound of waves lapping on the shore. The night before, we scouted about in the dark to find a spot to sleep and hide in. On the way there it was so dark, it was black, pitch black. As we drove I got so relaxed I fell asleep with the dog. In the morning Rick said what a trusting soul I was to fall asleep like that. I told him I was reminded of when Jesus was in the boat with the apostles and a storm came up and He was asleep. The apostles were afraid that they would perish. Jesus arose and rebuked the wind and the sea by saying "Peace, be still." I said He could only have done that because He knew He was going to the cross and nothing could take Him away before God's plan and purpose for Him was accomplished. No cancer, no disaster, no accident, no storm is going to take me or you out as long as we know God's plan and purpose.

About a couple of days after this realization I told our fellowship group I thought I knew my purpose. It bothered me that I said it with uncertainty. The Lord spoke to me later to confirm that I know my purpose. I've been called and anointed to heal the broken hearted, open the eyes of the blind, set the captives free, and preach the acceptable year of the Lord. We have a job to do. We are anointed of God to do this work and nothing can take us until God says its time. Set yourself firmly never being moved and know you're called and anointed by the spirit of the Most High God. Turn every eye on Him for He is greatly to be Praised.

I was watching T.V. one night and the Feed My Children program was feeding children in Bosnia. I got so emotional about these children I wanted to immediately go to Bosnia. I was so intense about going I was praying about how to sell things and get there. For two days I was very bored with everything. Everything felt out of joint. I knew something was wrong but figured it was getting me ready to go. I was experiencing God's anointing to pray for Bosnia.

I started thinking about Kathy and her baby. I had talked to her after the birth but not since her milk would have come in. So I decided to call her and see how she was. We chatted for a minute and then there was nothing on the other end of the phone. I thought the phone went dead but then I realized I was hearing crying. I said "Kathy, is something wrong? Do you want me to call back later"? She said in a very weak crying almost sobbing voice, "No. I guess I was just so surprised to hear your voice." She sobbed into the phone and I didn't know what to do. I began to cry also. We were both crying and strangely I knew it was not about me or her but we were so full of the Lord and what we were experiencing was the Lord's powerful anointing. It was just the sound of my voice that had caused it. We didn't try to explain it but we abided in it. We talked about baby and how the family was but at the end of the conversation Kathy began to cry again. I Praised the Lord and shared how much I knew He loved her and her family. God had touched her and was working in her as He used our time together to bring her to Him. I had no doubt that Kathy was wrapped in the anointing of salvation and wonderful things were happening.

Anointing is in us by the life of Jesus Christ. The same anointed Christ that walked in power and went about healing all that would receive. When Jesus died for us, He released the power of Pentecost, the Holy Spirit to every believer. When we receive the Baptism of the Holy Ghost we receive power from on high and we are then walking in anointing. The same anointing Jesus was walking in. We have anointing and power for everything. If you walk in love then this anointing breaks the yoke and smashes it to smithereens. Pray that people will receive this life of Christ and break up the fallow ground. Jesus said:

"Go your way and tell John what things ye have seen and heard, how the blind see, the lame walk, the lepers are cleansed, the deaf hear, the dead are raised, and to the poor the gospel is preached. And blessed is he. whosoever shall not be offended in me." Luke 7:2-23

Pray that the hearer is not offended in Jesus Christ. The parable of the sower of the seed in Luke chapter 8 explains why some don't receive.

I can't tell you all the stories of babies that were born not breathing and God's love, power, grace, mercy, light and sound held them and breathed into them His anointing. His life, I love being apart of His life and helping families realize how very close God is to them all the time. Turning to God instead of our own ways or the ways of the world, or what seems right. Trusting in God's love for us is so powerful. I feel crazy in the light of all God is and we can have it all in Him. There is so much waiting out there for us to shine in. Birth is a shinning place. That is why it always changes our lives.

Chapter 12

God's Keeping Power

That Christ may dwell in your hearts by faith; that ye, being rooted and grounded in love, May be able to comprehend with all saints what is the breadth, and length, and depth, and height; And to know the love of Christ, which passeth knowledge, that ye might be filled with all the fullness of God. Now unto him that is able to do exceeding abundantly above all that we ask or think, according to the power that worketh in us, Unto him be the glory in the church by Christ Jesus throughout all ages, world without end. Amen. Ephesians 3:17-21

It was winter, snowing very hard, and was very cold. I was working and remember thinking I'd like to just go home and sleep for a couple of days. My expectant mom called me and said "Do you mind coming over to check on me? I feel like I might be in labor." We had done one child together and she delivers pretty quickly so I told her I'd swing by after work.

Because of the snow it took a lot more time to get there. When I arrived. I could see she was not in labor. She was cooking supper and hadn't had a contraction for about 10 minutes. They weren't hard, no leaking of water or show so I decided to check her. She was 2 cm and 50% effaced. It could be any time but I didn't feel it was tonight so we visited. Baby was moving around a lot and the heart beat was great so I headed home. I got home at 10:00 p.m. I immediately put my pajamas on and relaxed with my husband, Rick. We had some dinner and it was still snowing a little.

The phone rang and it was my expectant mom. She was breathing hard and telling me this is it. I said, "Praise the Lord, I'll be right there." It was going to be an hour and a half drive in the snow "Yickes." I went to Rick who had fallen asleep on the couch and asked him if he'd mind driving me. He looked at me like I was crazy. I said, "I know you're really tired and besides I have the anointing for this not you." I was so

tired I really couldn't move but managed to get all my stuff together. Rick prayed over me and off I went at midnight into the cold, dark, snowy night.

I put my hands on the steering wheel and prayed, "God help me make it in time. Take care of mom and baby." About 10 minutes into the drive I started crying. Usually God comes in and takes over when I'm tired like this but this time I had to fight sleep and anger. "Why did I have to go tonight. I'm tired!" I cried. "Jesus help me." The visibility was terrible so I had to go really slow. I was about three quarters there and I got so sleepy I couldn't keep my eyes open. It was taking me twice as long to get there. My head dropped several times and hit the steering wheel. I was jolted awake every time and swerved. I was thankful no one else was on the road. I rolled the windows down and shouted and sang till I just couldn't keep my head up. I remember seeing the road go between 2 rock mountain ledges and I felt so safe. I just laid my head down on the wheel very gently and it felt so good to rest. I woke up driving into her driveway. I stopped abruptly because I was going to hit the inside of her carport. I had arrived and I had been asleep for about 30 minutes while supposedly driving.

I jumped out of the car and ran in the house. Everyone was in their bedroom and they turned and said her water just broke. I laughed and said, "Just in time, huh!"

Daddy caught the baby. I praised the Lord and marveled at what just happened. Was I transported? Did Jesus just take over the wheel and drive me there? What took place in that 30-40 minutes? I tell you it was the Supernatural Keeping Power of our Lord Jesus. He loves us, He cares for us. He saves and delivers.

Chapter 13

Praise and Worship

I will praise thee; for I am fearfully and wonderfully made. Marvelous are thy works and that my soul knoweth right well.
Psalms 139:14

When I first started in midwifery I only praised God after I saw the baby was alright or when answered prayer was seen. It was very much by sight. Oh how good the Lord is to teach and have grace over us when we're young. As I went step by step, line by line, and precept by precept, I learned to praise God for everything because He is worthy of all praise.

I've had couples call me years later after their birth and tell me that they can still hear me saying, "Thank you Jesus." I constantly thank Jesus at a birth. It's been something that gives me strength and keeps me focused on the great physician by calling on Him in time of need. Praise keeps applying pressure to the outcome.

I was at a birth of a couple who were not at all homebirth candidates. They were full of fear because they didn't know any better and they felt trapped to do a birth with me due to the lack of doctors and lack of money. I became intimidated when I saw their fear. I hadn't been around real fear in awhile. I started letting my mind wander and ideas of what ifs started happening.

Before I knew it, I was looking at problems. First the baby's heart beat was going down. Then the mother started screaming and that can really shake your ground. She was begging her husband to take her to the hospital. I got terrified and started to panic. I closed my eyes and cried out to the Father. He said, "Praise Me!" I thought Praise You? for what?

Then I heard the fear again and now it was time to obey! I started Praising God for everything. I praised God for the good and healthy baby, the heartbeat going normal, the mother being in perfect peace, a baby that screams when it's delivered, a perfect birth, and an easy delivery. I was thanking God for Jesus who made a way for us. I thanked God for Grace, strength, joy, and peace. Well that baby delivered and came out screaming even before the rest of its body was out. It was easy and the mother calmed down and even had some moments of peace and joy. Daddy was laughing and encouraging mom instead of biting his lip and shaking. Oh! What a difference it made Praising Him for the outcome and the promises. I especially praised God for his faithfulness to me, covering me, never leaving me nor forsaking me. THANK YOU FATHER GOD. GOOD AND MIGHTY GOD!

Praise cuts the path, pushes the mountain, builds a ladder, and hurdles you over the problem. Praise makes a bridge, flies above and shows you the enemy and how small he is and that there is more with you then with them. Praise stops your mind from thinking and meditating on the fear and the negative "what ifs." Praise is God's tool to stop the enemy.

"I will praise thee. O Lord, with my whole heart. I will show forth all thy marvelous works. I will be glad and rejoice in thee. I will sing praise to thy name. O thou most High. When mine enemies are turned back, they shall fall and perish at thy presence."

When you Praise the Lord you will begin to feel confident and that stops fear and doubt. That is building the spirit man and your mouth will speak out of confidence instead of fear.

I had two births in one day about 2 hours distance from each other. I was leaving one in Harrison when I got called to go to a birth in Springdale. A Hispanic couple was having their second child and their first child had been so easy and fun, I was confident this one would be too. I was very tired but I had called Rick and he reassured me I could do all things through Christ and I would be home before I knew it. It is wonderful to have such a supportive and praying husband. So, I arrived at their home and saw she was in active labor. I visited for awhile and then I felt I should check her and see how we were doing. I checked her and found baby was breech. It felt like a "frank breech" which is where the butt was coming first with legs folded against the baby's body. I couldn't communicate really well with the family because of our language differences but I tried to tell them what was going on and I could see they didn't grasp the situation. They responded with an attitude of "Ok, you will take care of this right?" I panicked. I went out to my car and called Rick again. He told me to calm down and take a deep breath. He prayed for me and encouraged me that God has never let me down. I got off the phone and still wasn't together. I felt really alone and tired. I knew the couple didn't know what we were facing and didn't have a real strong faith in the Lord.

    I guess I was so very down that I surprised myself, I needed God NOW. I wanted to call some midwives in the area but I left my address book at the house in Harrison at the other birth and they were not picking up. I sat in the car and cried. I had never felt so lost. I hated to take this couple to the hospital but I wasn't ready for the battle and the work a breech baby took. I sat quietly trying to figure out what to do. I heard a song, float up. Just a little song, "Trust in the Lord, He is mighty!" I heard more and then more. I dried my eyes and said a prayer for wisdom and courage. If Joshua in the Bible could do it then so can I.

    I went in the house and they looked at me like I was crazy. I must have looked awful because I had been up for over 24 hrs. I got things ready and tried to ask the couple if they wanted to go to the hospital. They said, "No, Nancy you deliver our baby, ok." Ok, my God I needed help and here came the song again and this time, some wisdom came with it. I instructed mama to not push. We were going to sit there until she just can't stand it and then push. Ok? Then I started singing. God gave me some wonderful songs. A tremendous peace and joy started to flow. The couple relaxed and she started to push a little. I would tell her, "Not yet", then sing some more songs. I got comfortable, everything was ready and then she couldn't keep from pushing. I had her squat and we all sang together. I don't know what they sang but it was nice and my praises went with theirs and eventually this little butt came out. Then I pulled the legs down and pulled up a little and the chest was born and then the baby's head came out. He was beautiful and cried right away so I laid him up on momma. She cried and I am sure she was relieved, I know I was. God was there.

Through His praises and presence this little baby was born. The feeling of pressure and warfare was overwhelming but through God's praises we came through beautifully. Thank You Father the Deliverer!

You're so sweet, so sweet to me
You're so sweet, so sweet to me
You set the moon in the night, for me
You set the sun in the day, for me
You hung the stars to twinkle, to me
You blew the breeze to give me, strength
So sweet, so sweet, So beautiful to me I praise you Lord
I worship thee!

Chapter 14

The Battle

The battle is on whether we want to be at war or not. We are in a battle at all times. In Ephesians 6, God instructs us to put on the whole armor of God. God has been revealing to me about the criticalness of wearing His armor and not taking it off. Jesus has bought and paid for this armor and He poured His blood out for the armor and tried it in the fire. There is only one armor, and when you put on the whole armor of God there is no division or doctrine. It is just one body, and one armor. Satan can not see the believer only the armor. You are totally protected and overcoming in the armor. Totally safe, walking in righteousness and truth, totally free and victorious! All that is required when you go to battle is to be suited up and walk in unity or in line. Be ready and remember, the battle is the Lord's! 1 Samuel 17:47

If we are not in the armor of God but in our own flesh we die. You cannot go into battle in the flesh. It must be a walk or war in the spirit.

We war not against flesh and blood, but against and principalities, against powers, against the rulers of the darkness of this world, against spiritual wickedness in high places. Ephesians 6:12

The Lord gave me a vision in intercessory prayer. He showed me the body of Christ suiting up into the armor and I heard the sound of the armor being put on by billions of Christians. Then I heard the body getting in line and beginning to march and the sound was awesome. It was thunderous and the ground was shaking. I saw that the shaking is the body of Christ getting in line with the will of God. I saw Satan and his hordes tremble and fall, literally crack up, run into each other and die. The battle is the Lord's and we are to be ready with God's armor on, get in line and march, always holding our ground and not being moved. Standing! This is the victory! A young woman with her mother came to me. She was five months pregnant and wanting to have a home birth. She had had a child when she was very young and gave the baby girl up for adoption. This had been a very emotional, hard birth for her due to a very traumatic c-section. She was really excited about this new pregnancy and very adamant about not having another c-section or hospital birth. She was very certain of her due date and was very healthy.

We began visits getting to know each other very well and I felt a lot of healing was occurring through the Lord. Her due date came and went. We were on edge waiting for baby. Week after week went by and no sign of labor or any indication she was going to birth anytime soon. Baby was high up and cervix wasn't opening, no mucus plug or contractions, nothing. Baby was very active and looking back I would say baby was the only one full of faith, but a battle went on in all of our minds.

Sometimes the real battle is all the *what ifs* in the mind. At two weeks overdue I began crying out. I could feel in the spirit something was up and to get ready to stand and with all that was within me stand some more. We were nearing 5 weeks and still waiting.

Wherefore take unto you the whole armour of God, that ye may be able to withstand in the evil day, and having done all, to stand. Ephesians. 6:13

"But let patience have her perfect work, that ye may be perfect and entire, wanting nothing. James 1:4

But let him ask in faith, nothing wavering. For he that wavered is like a wave of the sea driven with the wind and tossed. For let not that man think that he shall receive anything from the Lord. A double minded man is unstable in all his ways. James 1:6

My faith was really starting to waver and I was getting a

little crazy. I had lots of vain imaginations and what ifs going through my mind. The medical field has done such a trip on all of us about overdue babies. It is so hard to have faith for God's timing and trust that He who has started this good work will perform it. At this time I was forced to read the word night and day. This mommy was always on my mind. I found myself praying even in my sleep. I was so uneasy, asking prayer groups for prayer and losing my peace. I was seeing her often and doing non-stress tests and trying to find out what was holding everything up. On the morning of her birth I got up early and began crying out. I shouted to the Lord, "Birth her! keep baby safe and show me what to do." There was no where to go, no emergency room will take a woman who is not in labor so we were stuck literally. Was the baby stuck too? Dear Lord, no.

I had gotten on my harp and sang a new song to the Lord about how He watches over us and keeps us, never sleeps nor slumbers. I was feeling better after all that but still decided to call Jen. For the millionth time I was going to try to talk her into seeing a doctor or trying castor oil. Before I could call, Jen called me and she felt like she might be in labor. We squealed for joy on the phone but now the fun began. I could only hope baby was not in some weird position or that the labor would be too long and miserable for Jen and baby.

When I arrived much to my surprise, Jen was in the birth tub and her family was there. The atmosphere was peaceful and fun. Jen was in active labor and feeling like pushing. I couldn't believe my eyes. I started praising the Lord for His birthing and keeping power over baby and momma. I ran around singing and getting instruments together for cutting the cord. We were having a baby. Finally after waiting five weeks overdue, I had never had this happen. If I thought too much about it I would panic but I just kept singing and rejoicing.

Baby was born in the water. She was very wrinkly and had so much major skin peeling that I was really nervous about it. The next day they saw a pediatrician, a family friend, and he said she was certainly over due but just as healthy as could be. Praise God! A little girl, beautiful and so longed for. I was happy but also aware that the battle over this momma and baby was fierce and still think and pray for them often.

All of God's promises had to be brought to mind. We are constantly tempted to cave in and doubt. God is right there assuring us that we can trust Him and that the battle is His. We just have to show up. In 2 Sam.22, God gave David a song of deliverance, encouraging David to come to battle. It was the Lords battle and all David had to do was show up and God would put His foot on the neck of the enemy. David was to pulverize the enemy until he was dust. I believe that our minds must:

Take every thought captive that exalts itself above God, and cast down every vain imagination. 2 Corinthians 10:5. 2

As for God, His way is perfect; the word of the Lord is tried; He is a buckler to all those that trust him. For who is God, save the Lord? and who is a rock, save our God? God is my strength and power: and He maketh my way perfect. He maketh my feet like hinds feet; and setteth me upon my high places. He teacheth my hands to war; so that a bow of steel is broken by mine arms. Thou hast given me the shield of thy salvation; and thy gentleness hath made me great. 2 Samuel 22:31-36

I learned so much while waiting for this birth. God is good, trust Him and show up when He calls, ready to Praise Him.

The battle is on,
The battle is on
Come to the battle
The battle is on
Hear that sound
Victory in the air
Don't turn back
Victory isn't there
Come up higher
I Am there
Victory! Victory!
Stand with Me there!

Chapter 15

Trust

Blessed is the man that trusts the Lord. his confidence is in Him.
Jeremiah 17:7

Hope in the Lord. We that love the Lord must enter into a depth of trust that is not human. We cannot expect our human understanding of trust to be what God means to trust in Him. Out of fellowship and communion with Him we will find dialog to help us trust Him at levels that we have never been before. When we begin to trust and lean on God not on our own understanding but on His divine plan we will overcome the circumstances and expectations of people.

I had been talking to Ruth and Kyle for years by phone and yet had never met them. They live in Missouri and I do not have a license for that state so have not been able to attend their births. We have had two births discussed over the phone and much anointing has been there to see them through all the confusion at times. They wanted home births but ended up with a C-Section and a clinic birth with a non-Christian midwife. This time they really wanted a Christian midwife and they asked me if I would take them. I knew the State Health Department would not ok a baby at home after a C-Section but I knew we should try and believe God could make a way.

Ruth wrote letters and looked for Doctors to ok a birth at home for a vaginal birth after a c-section called a V-back but all doors were closed. The added problem was that I couldn't go into Missouri so I encouraged them to pray for a Godly midwife to appear for them. One did it seemed for a couple of months and then something happened and she had to back out. Normally this would have discouraged them and set in my mind an acceptance to going to the hospital but it didn't. I found myself ready to tell them one thing and then God would speak something else. There was so much encouragement to stand and believe God as the Mighty Deliverer and to trust with spiritual trust and not human. Soon they were 24 days late and they were getting nervous and I should have too according to what I had been taught in the world. I Thank God I'm learning more from God now and care less about the world. The scripture "He who loves the world does not love God." is starting to become real to me. I never understood that scripture until recently. If I'm so full of the word of God and hear and speak only what He says I will begin to reject the world and thus hate the world. I will be living in the kingdom.

    I told Ruth to wait on the Lord and hear from Him about everything. Don't just follow me, I told her, but find out what He wants from you. Two days later they called and she was appearing to be going into labor. I got full of the Joy of the Lord and couldn't help getting some on them. At 3 o'clock in the morning they called to tell me they were tired and disappointed that God had not delivered their baby yet. They were having a recurring thought or dread that the baby was transverse and wouldn't come. I thought, "O God" but said; "What is God saying to you? Where is your peace? This is not about God now, this is about what are you doing and what are you hearing." I told the daddy to check Ruth and see if there is a head down and if not pray about what God would want you to do. Does He want you to go to the hospital or what, but get in His peace. We hung up and I laid there wanting to go back to sleep or should I get up and intercede because this baby could be in big trouble. So I asked the Holy Spirit to be there with them and help them hear from God and what He wanted me to do. He said "Go to sleep. Everything is fine." And so I did.

    Twenty minutes later the phone rang and it was Kyle. I said "Oh Kyle what's wrong!" He said; "Listen"! I heard the baby crying. WOW! I started yelling Hallelujah and Praising God. Kyle said; "We prayed and God said to check her and there was the head so we pushed and she came out screaming and pink. The water broke when she pushed and no tares or even much blood.

I hung up and danced around the room happier than if I had been there. It is odd from a human point of view but it was better that only God be the Deliverer. He will be delivering me moment by moment forever and that is a Mightier and more Glorious picture than humanity always needing a Doctor's help. God is our Help and our All in All in whom we Trust. I talked with them several days later and they were learning so much. Kyle especially wanted to know how to hear the voice of the Lord because it had really bothered him that I asked, "What is God telling you?" It is their walk that is important to God. Not what we think or expect should happen but what He has called them to and the faith that they walk in everyday. Trust!

A dear friend of mine called me right after Christmas and told me about her surprise Christmas present to her husband. Sally had been having trouble with her period and was gaining weight and was worried something bad was wrong. She went to see the doctor and after seeing the ultrasound found out she was pregnant. She took the picture and wrapped it up for her husband for Christmas. He was shocked. The reason he was so shocked was they were not suppose to have anymore children since their motorcycle accident that left them both badly hurt many years ago. Sally's hip, side, legs and heart were badly damaged. Her heart was torn and had a patch on it.

Sally had always wanted a homebirth so she called to see what I thought. The whole story was a miracle and I heard the Lord say, "Help them find a way, trust Me." My better judgment told me to refer them but I knew it couldn't hurt to talk and pray about a plan. We all met and discussed our options. The plan was to have them see a doctor and midwife. I and another midwife would go with them to the hospital and help them have as close to a homebirth as they can. Sounded like a great plan.

During Sally's prenatal she had hypertension and was on bed rest. Sally said she was so happy to be pregnant. She never worried. She just stayed in bed a lot and read the bible. It was a time to be really close to the Lord. Her Doctor was great too. Cindy, my friend who is a midwife, and I prayed and consulted a lot together about her pregnancy. It was a little risky with her heart history and now high blood pressure. I got a call from Don, the husband, he was kind of anxious and said, "Sally has been having some labor all day and now she is saying this could be it." I said, "Ok, let's head to the hospital in Harrison, call the Doctor and I will be right behind you."

We hung up and I got dressed and the phone rang. It was Sally and she said I am coming over to your house for you to check me. I told her I think we should just go because we don't want to have a baby on the road. Sally was adamant that she stopped at my house first. I said "Ok, come on, I'll check her quick and then go."

Their friends, Shelly and Don, with their two children came to the house helping Sally. She obviously was in hard labor. The minute I saw her I got excited. I could see she was close, it was a wonderful feeling. They all still had their coats on when I checked her and found she was a complete ten centimeters, ready to go with a bulging bag of waters. I said "Well, we are not going anywhere, don't even get up off the bed the baby is coming." I then called the Doctor and Cindy, the other midwife, to tell them what was happening. I got some equipment out and sterilized some instruments. Katie, her daughter had the job of reading scriptures during the birth and so I said, "Lets get our coats off and Katie you can read and Charlie you can pray.

Don was busy calling family and just in shock. I kept looking up and seeing him walking around still with his coat on. All of a sudden Sally yelled, "My water just broke." Oh, boy here we go. I got her to get her dress up and looked and there was the baby coming. She just pushed a time or two and there was Chole. A beautiful big baby girl, screaming, pink and lively. Katie was still reading the bible. I believe she was reading in Revelations so I said, "Maybe psalms would be better." We all laughed. It was so joyful, so fast, so peaceful, wonderful and so trusting, that our Father had a plan. This was Sally's hearts desire and He delivered her perfectly. We all rejoiced and two hours later the family left to go home and we were all truly blessed. Blessed is the man that trusts in the Lord.

Chapter 16

Surrender

Begging God does not profit ever, only faith and resting. The only time striving is scriptural is:

Striving to enter into the rest. Hebrews 4: 11

Learning how to enter into the rest is the walk. It is hard until you totally trust God. Then you marvel at how simple and fun it is to learn to rest. For the last three years every time I ask the Lord to tell me how a birth will go. He always has said; "Be joyful. Everything will be fine. Have fun." I have struggled with this because it just isn't always fun. Lately I've been finding myself stepping out into faith and making a conscious effort to have fun and not be so serious and medical. I'm becoming very relaxed and this is helping the family. It especially helps the mother to relax and surrender faster to accept her work or labor. When we are at rest we can meditate and focus on the word. This brings truth and the truth sets you free, causing liberty. Real anointing and faith rise up and we find ourselves surrendered and in agreement with God's word. We are linked to the power and mightiness of Almighty God.

Nothing is impossible with God. Luke 1:37

I have seen a lot of women try to control their births and fight themselves and God. It is so painful to watch and to physically be a part of. I would be totally worn out until I learned to discern what the mom was doing. I would back off and start praying for her, speaking the word offering very little help in the physical realm as she cried. This seemed cruel at first until I learned that this was the fastest and least painful way to help her come to a place of surrender. Praying in the spirit quietly is the most effective help there is.

When surrender comes it is so sweet as everyone relaxes and you can feel the freedom. Things begin to look good again and actually fun. To stay in a place of control causes real bondage and fear lurks there. This is the danger zone. Letting fear abide with you begins to change everything and there is no rest, no peace, no fun, no power, no anointing.

Perfect love casts out fear. 1 John 4:18 I have not a spirit of fear but of love, power and a sound mind. 2 Tim 1:7

I have watched births go from joyful to sorrowful just because we indulged in control and not surrender. Surrender means to let go of your way. Let the word of God take authority by surrendering to God and His word. I could see with my eyes the progress being made. The cervix opens from one centimeter to ten in a matter of minutes. Rest and peace sweep over a crying tormented mother to weep tears of joy. Confusion leaves and the sweetest peace you can actually smell, like roses begin to fill the air. I can sense God's love and faithfulness and never changing mercy. I get energized and I realize what a strength God is in weakness. I always want to learn to do this faster the next time. I realize how simple it all seems in the moment and yet I find patience needs to have its perfect work. Yes!

Alice and Tom's first birth experience was awesome. Trust was everywhere. I had been out of town and they were two and a half weeks early when her water broke. It took me seven hours to get there and baby came two hours after I got there. Another midwife and doula, (a midwife aide) helped them through the night, and during the birth, bless them. The atmosphere was full of the Lord and Alice was so relaxed and trusting. Usually I have to say, "Relax, surrender to God," but not this time I felt she was totally in His hands.

When Alice got to nine centimeters an anterior lip hung on the baby's head. This lip can swell and can be painful, making the labor harder and more painful, a real trouble. I told Alice what was going on and that I might have some lobelia tincture, an herb that would help. While I was getting that, Alice just put her head down and prayed, "Dear God, please take the lip away." It was so sweet and faith filled the room. She surrendered and soon she was pushing. Baby Samuel was born in the water. He swam out and into our arms. We laid him on her chest and proceeded to suction the baby. The bulb syringe was not a good one and wouldn't suck in. I tried to maneuver him getting in a head down position to drain fluids out of his mouth but the water was so full in the tub that I kept getting his head too near the water. The cord was not long enough to make this happen. Daddy said, "What's wrong?" I told him I needed baby to cough up some stuff in his lungs. Next thing I hear is daddy praying, "Thank you Lord for helping Samuel cough up the fluid." Immediately Samuel started coughing up fluid and we all rejoiced and laughed at the simplicity of faith and surrender. How sweet that God was so present and awesome, you could almost touch the Lord. Wouldn't have missed this for anything and I didn't, thank you Lord, you are a faithful God!

> Songs of sweetness in the air
> You are present everywhere
> Standing close your love so rare
> I feel your presence everywhere
> Sweet, sweet Lord
> Sweet, sweet Lord
> Come nearer
> Sweet, sweet Lord
> Sweet, sweet Lord
> Come nearer
> I am standing
> Waiting here
> Love is in the air!

Chapter 17

Overcoming Fear

"For God hath not given us a spirit of fear, but of power, and of love, and of a sound mind." 2 Timothy 1:7

FEAR IS PERVERTED FAITH! Satan rules with fear. He attacks our minds and keeps us holding on to our thinking instead of renewing our minds to God's promises and God's way of life. Satan tries to keep us in the past with what we know which is self righteousness. Jesus has a new and living way.

In the very beginning of my journey with the Lord's families and babies, I got an amazing challenge in overcoming fear. I was awakened in the night, by a phone call from one of my mothers that her bed was full of blood and what should she do. I was half asleep so I just started praying in the spirit very loudly and then I commanded all bleeding to stop and death to leave, in Jesus Name! I told her to go back to sleep, she'd be alright. The next morning I was totally oblivious of that phone call, not in my memory at all, this happens a lot to me after I have prayed for something. I really don't think of it again and isn't that the way it really is? It is taken care of so why ask again.

I was driving to work that afternoon and this dread and fear came all over me and almost made me sick. I pulled the car over and sat for a minute as I remembered the phone call I had late that night. I turned white with fear, my ears were ringing, oh my God what had I done. I should have called 911 for her. She might be dead and for sure her baby could be. I ran to a phone booth and called Diane. I was shaking with the fear that had gripped me. She said hello so sweetly! I yelled, "Are you alright? Are you still bleeding? I should have called an ambulance for you last night." She said, "Why? Right after you prayed the bleeding stopped and I felt fine."

The devil is a liar! Fear is not from God. The only kind of fear to have is Godly fear which is the respect and reverence of God, knowing He is sovereign and the beloved. I still knew the battle was on for her because at every prenatal check I couldn't hear the heart beat of the baby. In those days we didn't have doplers so I had to use my fetoscope. It is sometimes difficult to get a heartbeat with just a fetoscope. So we continued on, baby was growing according to her due date. She said she felt movement so we prayed. When the bleeding had occurred she was about five months and the whole time I never heard a heartbeat. Usually I would do something, but I didn't have any unction to send her anywhere or worry about it.

So the day comes when Diane goes into labor. I arrive and she is in hard labor. It was a strange labor because every contraction she yelled to her husband, "Lindel, pray the word now!" So, Lindel would pray scripture over her until the contraction ended and she would rest then jump up again and yell, "Lindel pray the word now!" God bless Lindel, he got a work out during that birth.

I felt fear trying to take hold of us. I was praying a lot, singing in the spirit, talking to God, and asking Him what was going on. Every time I tried to listen for a heartbeat I couldn't hear it. Diane would jump up with another contraction. Finally she got to pushing. She pushed hard and out came a baby girl. She was totally white, very thin, not much movement and hardly any sign of life. The cord was weird looking and the pulse in it had stopped. I lifted baby up onto momma's tummy and immediately Diane was talking to her baby and loving her. Really this was the first time Diane connected to anything since she started into labor. She was so inward the whole time, it was good to see her connect with the baby.

Baby's color was pinking up from the navel cord area. I had never seen this so I was in awe, praying out loud in the spirit and commanding life when I looked down on the bed a saw a lot of blood pouring out of Diane. I realized the cord was cut so I tugged a little on the cord and it broke, I was shocked. Now fear started to grip me but I heard the Lord say, *"Trust me, everything is alright"*. I said to Lindel, "Pray!" He immediately prayed loudly. I kept looking at Diane and she was so calm and talking to her baby, who by now was pink and looking around, which I was in awe of. Blood still coming I cried out Ezekiel 16:6 over and over.

Yea, though I lie polluted in my own blood I say live.

Every time I said Ezekiel 16:6 the bleeding stopped. Literally it would go from spraying blood to no bleeding at all. So I just kept saying Ezekiel 16:6. I finally got Diane to push the placenta out. It was tricky because we had no cord to maneuver but it came and when I saw it I just couldn't believe it. The placenta was white and hard. I continued to watch Diane and baby. They were locked on to each other. Even when Diane was bleeding I kept asking her if she was alright. She surely should have passed out with that much blood loss, but she was very alert and talking to her new baby who was now very pink and lively.

I remembered saying through out the whole pregnancy, "This baby is fearfully and wonderfully made, lively, healthy, full of Jesus' love and keeping power." So now momma and daddy are checking out their baby and I am in the bathroom taking a look at the weird placenta. It was totally white and calcified, (which is a lack of nutrition. If really calcified it means a dead placenta). The cord broke because it was deteriorated and there was no life in it. I looked in the mirror where I was washing the placenta off and saw myself. My face was white. I think I got gray hair that day, really. I said, "Oh, my God, this birth and baby are a miracle."

We all praised the Lord and danced around in total awe of what God just did. We prayed over the family and I stayed a long time. I guess I was just in shock at what had just taken place. On the way home, I felt like I was starting to come to. Come to the reality of what happened, what did happen? I asked the Lord, "Why didn't you tell me this was going to happen," He said, "You wouldn't have gone to the birth, and this would have happened." He suddenly put up a movie projector and screen.

When I was first a Christian, God would do this all the time. He would show me things by using a projector and movie screen. He showed me when Diane first called me and she was bleeding, that I would have run her to the hospital. The Doctors would have pronounced her baby dead and end of story. I cried tears of joy and amazement for such a God I serve. I really trusted in the unknown, just totally in the Lord. God is faithful to save and to deliver. For weeks after this birth I questioned and got afraid, what if this happens again? The Lord assured me it would.

This I can only explain is the mystery of God choosing the foolish things of the world to confound the wise.

God hath chosen the weak things of the world to confound the things which are mighty. And base things of the world, and things which are despised, hath God chosen, yea, and the things that are not, to bring to naught things that are: That no flesh should glory in his presence. But of him ye are in Christ Jesus, who of God is made unto us wisdom, and righteousness, and sanctification, and redemption: That, according as it is written, HE THAT GLORIETH, LET HIM GLORY IN THE LORD. 1Corth. 1:27-31

Everyday I have to overcome fear of some sort. Satan is roaring about looking for whom he may devour.

Casting all your care upon him; for he careth for you. Be sober, be vigilant; because your adversary the devil, as a roaring lion, walketh about, seeking whom he may devour; whom resist steadfast in the faith, knowing that the same afflictions are accomplished in your brethren that are in the world. But the God of all grace, who hath called us unto his eternal glory by Jesus Christ, after that ye have suffered a while, make you perfect, stablish, strengthen, settle you. "To him be glory and dominion for ever and ever. Amen"
1Peter 5:7-11

In the midst of all trials which is what this life really is, I take my favorite scripture God always gives me when I ask for a word;

"For God hath not given me a spirit of fear, but of power, and of love, and of a sound mind." 2 Timothy 1:7

"Faith cometh by hearing and hearing by the word of God". Romans 10:17

It has helped me to know the difference between facts and truth. Facts are what we see, and yes, we have to deal with them, but truth is WHAT IS! So how do we find truth? If all you know is the world's truth then that is all you will get. If you know God and study His word and live and move and have your being in Him, then you will experience the supernatural. I would pray that whoever is reading these life experiences will want more than the world can offer and dive into the Lord Jesus. He is King! He is Deliverer! He is salvation! He is love! He is life!

Right now, you can decide! Do you want just the world and it's knowledge or do you want to go for the true knowledge and truth. God has created a way, now say, "Father show me how to walk in it." This is the way the Father has shown me, even living on the edge. If I trust in Him I can only fall into His hands. David in the old testament had to face himself and his humanness. He had sinned and he was given a choice by the prophet: Let the armies of the enemy have you or three years of famine or put yourself in the hands of the living Lord. David in all his humanness knew God and knew that God's wrath and justice were so much more alive and loving than anything the world had to offer. He knew if he had to choose, the Father's love would cover him and keep him, even unto death. *2 Sam. 24:12-14*

It is the truth! I can say this from experience. He is always there to comfort, guide, humble, breathe life into me, raise me up, forgive, strengthen, spin joy over me, to promote, prosper, help, bless me and my family, keep me from harm, show me His goodness and to reveal the truth to me. God would never hurt me or forsake me. If you still question what is the truth, God says He is the truth, the light, and the way. If you doubt this, ask the Lord for wisdom and understanding and He will reveal truth {Jesus Christ} to you.

If any man lacketh wisdom let him ask of the lord and He will give it liberally and up braideth you not. James 1:5

I, like King David, would rather be in the Lords hands than the hands of man. Do not be afraid of what man thinks or can do to you. Follow the living Lord and you will not be ashamed. He will give you courage to follow the truth, His will.

Being confident of this very thing, that he which hath begun a good work in you will perform it until the day of Jesus Christ. Philippians 1:6

Even with all the trials and tribulations the Kingdom of God is still the most wonderful, peaceful, powerful, loving place, on this earth. I choose God's way. It is perfect. Read *Psalms 19*.

Rest!
Don't think about tomorrow
Rest!
I've got your back tomorrow
Rest!
Think sweetness not sorrow
Rest!
My love has covered you
Rest!
Best times ahead of you
Rest!
I'll be with you
Rest!

Chapter 18

Imaginations

"But I beseech you, that I may not be bold when I am present with that confidence with which I think to be bold against some who think of us as if we walked according to the flesh. For though we walk in the flesh, we do not war after the flesh. For the weapons of our warfare are not carnal but mighty through God to the pulling down of strongholds, Casting down imaginations and every high thing that exalteth itself against the knowledge of God and bringing into captivity every thought to the obedience of Christ; And having in all readiness to punish all disobedience when your obedience is fulfilled, Do you look on things after the outward appearance. If any man trust to himself that he is Christ's, let him of himself think this again, that as he is Christ's, even so are we Christ's." 2 Corinthians 10:2.

Since I became born again I have been given a vivid imagination. There have been times when I questioned some of the things I saw or thought were God and missed some of the value and the faith to believe what God was showing me. I see now that just as there is a Godly spiritual side to everything in life there are also counterfeits. Vain imaginations are one of those counterfeits.

It clearly states in 2 Corinthians 10:5 that we should cast down vain imaginations. That's because God has His imaginations He wants us to pursue. The reason that the flesh or carnal is troubled by vain or useless imaginations is that God has something powerful to give us if we would just abide in Him. I believe this God given kind of imagination is so powerful it gives substance to faith.

> *"Faith is the substance of things hoped for,*
> *the evidence of things unseen." Heb 11:1*

Giving substance to faith is living in resurrection power and letting our spirit with His direct our life. Abiding in God and believing that God has given us this wonderful, creative imagination for the purpose of abiding and walking in faith is exciting. So wouldn't something this exciting of God be quite a target for the devil? How he fools us is to let us believe that the earthly or carnal imaginations like doubt, unbelief, fear, worry, self preoccupation and grandeur are normal or acceptable thought patterns. We even build a whole medical practice of psychiatry around all the neuroses.

We have bought a lie. The lie is so big and so deep it even goes generational. I guess we could trace this lie all the way back to the Garden of Eden. Eve was having vain imaginations about what God was keeping from her. She probably entertained a thought from Satan and mulled it over until it rose up so big it outweighed all the love and fellowship our Father was having with her. This fellowship would have been awesome so you know it would have been a pretty powerful imagination that caused the death of our spiritual relationship with God our Father.

We have that same fellowship as Eve did before her fall because of what Jesus did for us. How we lose the fruits of the spirit is by entertaining vain, lying, and preoccupying thoughts. Letting them exalt themselves above our very fellowship with God. These are strongholds that are keeping us from the real work of our Father, which is: *To believe on the one God sent. John 6:29.*

Jesus wants us to use all He has given us and create with our imagination the Kingdom of God. Even the statements: "The Kingdom of God," and "Thy Kingdom come," are the very creative ideas that have been planted in your heart. God obviously wanted us to believe them and have faith that the Kingdom of God could be in our heart. When God says come boldly into the throne room of grace, he's asking us to use our God given imagination and obtain grace.

When I look around and see all the wonderful creations of God I'm amazed at how awesome and purposeful God is. He didn't set His creation up with such diversity and then not want us to use all He is when we abide in Him. With the Holy Spirit's direction and leading He will show us everything Jesus is and was and will be.

> *"All things that the Father hath are mine; therefore said I, that he shall take of mine and shall show it unto you." John 16:15*

He will show us by His word which is so imaginative and powerful. He will show us by His fellowship.

> *"Coming boldly into the throne room of grace that we may obtain mercy. and find grace to help in time of need." Heb. 4:16*

He will speak to us. To even believe that He will speak to us is to have a faith-filled imagination. When we abide in God, it pulls down strongholds of accepted carnal behavior and leaves an open door for faith. For when our imaginations are abiding in God, faith is released. It then becomes seen and spoken taking on substance and form.

> *"what so ever you ask of God, God will give it thee." John 11:22.*

Pull down those strongholds! Unleash the creative power of God. Believe in the spirit of God. Don't believe the lie. Abide in God and be ready to see and believe all He is, and was, and will be. Jesus said:

> *"Verily, verily, I say unto you. He that believeth on me, the works that I do shall he do also, and greater works than these shall he do, because I go unto my Father." John 14:12.*

Now imagine that! About ten years ago I was working for home health and going to bible school learning all kinds of new faith levels. I had trouble believing for alcoholics to be healed but I could believe for physical healings. I was called to the home of one of the patients. This was an old woman with an alcoholic son named Joshua. We received a call and Joshua was crying hysterically. We thought his mother had died. When I arrived I saw his mother and she was fine but Joshua was so slobbering drunk that he was crying and complaining that no one loved him. It turns out no one could stand his drunken behavior and all his kids had disowned him and his wife had left him years ago.

I felt disgust for the spirit of alcohol but God showed me compassion for the man. He was in torment. I cried out to the Lord to show me how to minister with this spirit present. The Lord said.

"Bind up the spirit of alcohol and give him a word to hold on to"

I found an old dusty bible and opened to:

"Submit yourselves therefore to God. Resist the devil and he will flee from you. Draw near to God and he will draw near to you."
James 4:7

Joshua prayed with me and repented of his sins. I left and never thought about whether he received or not I just left it in the Lord's hands. About two months later one of the nurses came in and told how she had heard Joshua was dying in the hospital from liver failure and the doctors and nurses said it was the worst case they had ever seen. Bile was coming out of his body onto the bed. It was a miserable situation. They all said "Poor Joshua." It really shook me because I had prayed and believed and I knew God was working. So what was happening?

That next day we had intercessory prayer at church and while we were praying Joshua came to mind. All I could believe for was to ask God to let Joshua see the victory. He had always failed in the past and never knew Jesus had won such a victory for him. I prayed, "God don't let Joshua go with out seeing the victory. Don't let his life be a total failure." Suddenly, I saw Joshua running in a race. He wasn't running though, he was crawling, and people were stepping on him and laughing at him. I began to cry and asked the others running in the race if we could help him, carry him, better yet drag him along holding his arms up to feel the victory. They all agreed and we ran with him around and around the track. Everyone got excited and cheered us on. Joshua was getting strength and a smile was coming on his face. I felt so sure this was helping. There were three of us interceding and we all stood up and clapped and shouted. "Joshua's going to make it." We crossed the finish line and we fell on each other as if it really happened. We had made it and Joshua had won. We lay on the floor and basked in God's love, sure it was done.

About two days later one of the nurses said. "Did you hear about Joshua? He has miraculously recovered from the liver failure and they're sending him home in a couple of days." I was shocked. I had totally let go of the prayer and now I was excited beyond anything I could think. I had to hear what had happened.

Joshua was home now so I went to visit. When I arrived he was in his chair and looked very yellow and thin. He had this smile on his face and I knew this smile. It was the Lords. It was a spiritual smile. I said, "What happened? I've been praying for you and I can see this is God's work. Please tell me what has happened." He then began to tell me how he was hovering over his body and saw what a miserable state he was in. He didn't think he was dying but he looked like he was. A nurse came in and he asked her. "Am I dying"? She said, "Yes." He asked if she would get a minister. Soon a man came in with a collar on like a minister and he knew they had gotten him one. The minister asked him, did he know Jesus? He said he didn't but wanted to. The minister told him he could just repent of his sins and say yes to Jesus. Joshua said, "I did that and the next thing I remember was I was awake and doctors and nurses were asking me how did I feel and did I know that I almost died." His liver function tests were normal but they didn't understand it. It appears he was healed or a miracle has happened. They were all shaking their heads and saying; "Well, he will probably relapse but he sure does look like he'll live today."

Joshua asked where the minister was and that he wanted to talk to him. No one knew who the minister was. None of them had had time to call one. Joshua started to get excited. He knew that must have been an angel and now he wanted to go home. Of course no one wanted him to. They said he was very weak and he could just relapse. Joshua said; "I knew I was healed and I felt great. I felt like telling everyone I was going to make it." He was smiling.

I was crying and proceeded to tell Joshua how we had prayed and imagined him going across the finish line. Joshua cried and asked if I would pray with him, that he would go tell all the drunks on the street that they could have this healing and happiness. Joshua was a brick layer and he wanted to lay brick again. A long time ago he started drinking and lost his family when he had hurt his back and had to go on disability. I hesitated to agree with him about the brick laying but I did because he looked so hopeful and I remembered the images of the race and how good that finish line was. So I prayed with him.

About three months later I went by his house and saw him laying brick at the neighbor's house. I honked my horn and he turned and smiled. He had that same big and sure spiritual smile.

Chapter 19

Impossible For Man

A dear family, I have known for years, had a great touch from the Lord. They were expecting again. We had three of their six children together and fellowshipped with them. Shawn, the daddy, had been attacked with pneumonia that turned into pericarditis and he ended up in the hospital. We visited and prayed and agreed with them on his victory over the circumstances. Sheri had a miscarriage in January so we weren't sure when she got pregnant again or when the baby was due. We trusted the Lord completely for all prenatal care and the timing of the birth. Because of Shawn's illness Sheri had to travel a lot to be with him so we just trusted the Lord to work out the details.

Many people were very concerned for them since the situation seemed kind of uncertain and they were definitely in a trial. I felt totally at peace with the trial and knew I was to support and intercede and encourage everyone involved. I was praising God everyday for the victory through the blood of Jesus and pleading the blood over the baby and the family.

Shawn got out of the hospital on Friday. Early the following Wednesday morning Sheri called. She said she woke up with pain in the vaginal area and a lot of bleeding she had never had before with any of the other births. It was tempting to get a little worried since I couldn't see what was happening and it could have been placenta previa, (when the placenta is partially or completely over the cervix opening). I asked the Lord to show me what they needed prayer for. God said, *"They will be fine and I am with them. Trust me and look to me for everything you need."* So all the way there I prayed in the spirit and praised the Lord. I got really happy by the time I arrived and if I started to get nervous I would just praise the Lord and I'd get perfect peace. I was marveling at how calm and happy I was.

I was so happy to see them. I just refused to believe that they were not blessed of the Lord in a trial or not. I checked Sheri to see if she was dilating since she wasn't having regular contractions but just pain and blood. Much to my surprise I felt a bulging bag of water and a dilated cervix to five and something moving that felt like fingers. I laughed and felt very excited and yet at peace. I knew this might mean twins or it could be feet. Oh boy, nothing was certain and everything was iffy. Well, I shared the possible good news with them and we just looked at each other trying to decide what to do. My body felt unusually calm and I was very happy so I started praising the Lord again.

I said something about whether they wanted to go to the hospital or call an ambulance but it was half hearted and it seemed very out of place. Shawn and Sheri were praising God too. We studied the situation and pondered, did we know what to do if it were twins or hands? Would we just pull them out and make way for the baby? We got excited to see baby. Sheri got up to go to the bathroom and I made a few phone calls. One to my husband to have him get a book for me to review. I asked him to pray and agree with me that God was totally in control and nothing should by any means hurt us because we were more than conquerors through Christ Jesus.

While I was drawing strength from Rick, Sheri got back in bed and her water broke. There were two little blue feet. Wow! Praise God! We all started praising God, thanking Him for mercy and life and victory through Jesus Blood. I asked Sheri what she felt I should do. She said "I have to push."

I said to myself, *"Dear Lord I can't do this"*!

He said,*"Good, I will do it. What is impossible with men is possible with God."*

I was very calm and yet my mind was saying things like,

"Maybe the baby isn't alive, How will I get his or her head out? I don't remember what I'm supposed to do and we should be in a hospital. But then I remembered God said; *"It's impossible for man but not for God"!*

"O.K. Sheri push!" I took hold of the little blue feet and pulled when she pushed. I pulled up and baby's belly and chest came out. Then I said if you can push go ahead and out came baby's head with a scream. Baby was screaming and we were screaming, "PRAISE THE LORD!"

We laid baby on momma's tummy and Shawn and I hit the floor and wept with joy and went into intercession. I felt the Holy Spirit was in total control. Sheri said. "This was the easiest birth I've ever had and her face showed the Glory of God! We continued to bask in the presence of the Holy One. We were abiding in grace and scripture was all we could talk to each other about. There was a unity that was very special and we knew that God had touched us. Life was abundant and we lacked for nothing. I felt a surety that we would never have to worry ever again. God was not slack toward us and nothing was impossible for God. He was able! Oh! Baby was a fat nine pound baby girl. They named her Johnna Grace. How wonderfully made she was. THANK YOU LORD.

On the way home it began to pour down rain. I felt so close to God with no separation. I asked Him to talk to me. God said,

"If you will look to me first in every situation, I will always deliver you. You will never have to fear. Don't run anywhere but to me. I will never leave you or forsake you. Trust me." Have not a spirit of fear but of love and power and a sound mind." 2 Timothy 1:7

Chapter 20

Intercession

Put on the whole armor of God that ye may be able to stand against the wiles of the devil. Ephesians 6:11 Confess your faults one to another, and pray one for another, that you may be healed. The effectual fervent prayer of the righteous availeth much. James 5:16

I wasn't even a Christian two years when God called me to intercession. I felt like I have always, even as a child, desired to pray like God showed me in the word. We lived out on the Kings River in Arkansas. It was beautiful out there. There was an old barn with a loft and a big open window. I would go everyday and sit in that window and the Lord would show me how to pray. I had some amazing times with the Lord, looking out over the pasture and seeing the beautiful bluffs along the river. Sometimes I long for that kind of time again, time to pray and sit with the Lord and seek Him till I find Him.

I had a job as a home health nurse for twenty years. I literally drove all over Madison County and met hundreds of old timers that moved to this country to make a new life for themselves with God. These elderly folks sure could pray. They would tell me stories of hearing prayer warriors all over the hill tops outside praying loudly, crying out to God for help for each other and their families. How they would get up before dawn and go outside even in the snow and heat and sit on a log and pray with their father or mother. I would pray with these folks and we would touch heaven.

While I was traveling around for those twenty years, I was

praying, singing, praying in the spirit, crying, listening, and shouting. What a job I had. I learned a lot from the Father in those years. If I wasn't talking to God, He was talking to me. One year the Lord told me to take a year off of work. I loved nursing and seeing these people in their homes and praying for them, I said "No." Well, it wasn't long before times got tough and I was confused and wondering what was going on. I sought the Lord and He said, *"You need to obey me."* I knew immediately that I was avoiding the Lord and His plan for me. I wasn't trusting Him. So, I talked with Rick about all this and he felt we should trust God and take a year off and follow God's leading.

That was a tough year, especially for the kids. It's hard for children to understand what a parent might need. It affected all of us, but now that I look back it was a pivotal year for my life. I now live totally by faith. I couldn't even imagine living like that 30 years ago. To trust the Lord for your work, provision, your health, and your life, is the best life there is. Intercession is essential. It is learning to listen to God , see in the spirit, meditate on the word, sing and prophecy, rest, shout and declare the things of God. I thought God would just teach me intercession but I had to live in it. I had to*: Press everyday for the mark of the high calling. Phil. 3:14*

The depths of intercession were awesome. I was finding God in every area of life knowing I could do nothing apart from Him. Over 900 births were physically and emotionally birthed in me too. I've learned God wants me to walk with Him like Enoch in the cool of the day. Walking together, talking, enjoying each other's company no matter what is happening around them. The joy of living and moving in the Fathers being, hearing His heartbeat.

I have found that worship is the highest form of intercession and sometimes I think I could worship 24/7. I thank God for our worshippers that get together every week. This time together is real unity of spirit. We explore heaven and it's like a big treasure hunt with God. He loves showing us his house, His dominion, His heart, His people, His victory, His sounds, His light, Son and spirit. We see things and declare things God shows us. He fills us with compassion. I believe we are transformed during these soakings with God. We sit for hours singing freely in the spirit, riding the heavens. We will never exhaust this Kingdom. God is fun, pure joy, pure love and I can't seem to get enough of Him. This is intercession, immersed in love, unashamed and unafraid to shout out His love and our devotion to Him. I was born to be this free and I am ruined for Him. We wait on Him to reveal Himself just like a birth. Constant waiting. I asked the Lord, "What shall we do while we are waiting for you to return?" He said, "*BIRTH*". Intercession is birth, come into it!

About five years ago, the Lord showed me I needed intercessors to pray for the ministry of birth. I asked friends and intercessors to stand with me in prayer for all my couples. Sometimes I give them names and due dates, sometimes I call them to ask for special prayer and sometimes my friends will call me and tell me they were praying for me or couples in the night or during the day. I believe we need to surround ourselves with the prayers of the saints. We are in the body and we need each other. I know it can not be done without one another.

I also see, and call on the angels to assist me in intercession. They are ministering spirits that we can call on them to come to our aid and help us.

for it is written, he shall give his angels charge over thee, to keep thee, and in their hands they shall bear thee up, lest at any time thou shalt dash thy foot against a stone. Luke 4:10

Jesus answered and said unto him, because I said, unto thee, I saw thee under the fig tree, believest thou? Thou shalt see greater things than these. And he saith unto him, verily, verily, I say unto you, Hereafter ye shall see heaven open, and angels of God ascending and descending upon the son of man. John 1:50

I often see the angels and especially at births. I asked the Lord one night what the name of these angels were and He said, "Birth angels." Of course, I love how the Lord deals with us.

Angels! Angels! crowding in
What do you see?
Glory! Glory! Everywhere, what a Glory be!

Jesus love is in the air
He must be here!
Looking for the one we love
It's just the humans full of love
Oh! wait, He is here
Arms open wide
He must really love them
He even died
But now we see
His love is all over thee
They act and talk just like him
Is it him or is it them?
Crowd in, I want to see
Is it him or is it them?
Come closer to me

Chapter 21

Joy

"The joy of the Lord is my strength." Nehemiah 8:10

This verse from Nehemiah is a reminder of what God wants us to trust in. He wants for us to remain in the spirit. I was praying with a dear friend and we asked the Holy Spirit to tell us what the church was? He answered;

"Little lights, shinning as a very bright light."

We saw Jesus' strong legs and feet. We were clinging to His leg just like a child does to his daddy when playing. Jesus was moving very fast and He said;

"This is the move of the spirit."

We felt like we might not be able to hold on we were moving so fast. Jesus then said,

"The joy of the Lord is your strength. If you hold fast to the spirit with joy then the fruit of the spirit will be manifest. When this fruit of love, joy, peace, patience, longsuffering, meekness, kindness, humility and faith manifests, it will annihilate the darkness. You will not see this because you will be in the light and it is the light that annihilates the darkness. When you're seeing the darkness you are not in the light for the light annihilates the darkness. I, God do not see the darkness because I am the light. Don't look upon or focus your attentions to the darkness for this is not being in the light. Look up, run to me, have your being in me. Hold fast to the faith and let the joy of the

Lord be your strength. The fruit will manifest and the light will surround you and you will not see the darkness."

I asked the Holy Spirit what discernment is. He said:

"Seeing the truth with love."

Then a song came forth. "Peace, be still and know that I am God." He showed us we were seeds planted in a hostile planet. He was the rain and He filled us with His will. Light poured forth from us and annihilated the darkness. While we sang we felt such a dear presence of the Lord. He gave us an image of our form as maybe He sees us. It was beautiful in a light and peaceful way. We realized God doesn't see our darkness. He perceives what He fearfully and wonderfully made. Here is a wonderful reference for all we learned of the Lord that day. We had much peace and joy and I felt I had the strength to hold on.

Clothe yourselves therefore, as God's own chosen ones (His own picked representatives), who are purified and holy and well-beloved by God Himself, by putting on behavior marked by tenderhearted pity and mercy, kind feeling, a lowly opinion of yourselves, gentle ways, and patience which is tireless and long-suffering, and has the power to endure whatever comes, with good temper. Colossians 3:12

Joy comes in the morning. So many, many mornings I have been filled with the joy of a baby coming after a hard night's work, waiting to birth, so wanting to see the baby, see the dawn. I often feel it is like waiting for Jesus to return. When, Lord, when? We are waiting for you. The Lord always tells me He is waiting for us! The joy we are both going to have when we are together again. I get it now though in small glimpses, unspeakable joy.

When I first started helping with babies, I asked the Lord to tell me what was the most important thing to learn about birth? He said, "*Joy!*" I look for Joy at every birth. I look for joy even at the birth's that are not a physical birth, like a child being birthed out of rebellion or some friend being birthed from an attack on their body. About ten years ago the Lord told me to believe for multiple births at each birth. Use the birth of a baby to birth ideas like birthing people into the Kingdom of God or a closer relationship with their spouse or birth into a deeper walk with Him. So you see we are always birthing. Paul said,

> *"My little children, of whom I travail again until Christ be formed in thee." Gal 4:19*

In these last days Joy is probably the one fruit of the spirit that is lost the easiest. Remember Joy is our strength according to Neh.8:10. I pondered what birth story to share here and what I got was, all of them. Whether it is an easy birth or a hard birth, they are all counted with Joy. This scripture is another one the Lord has always given me when I ask for a word.

count it all joy when you fall into various trails and tribulations ; knowing this, that the trying of your faith worketh patience and let patience have her perfect work." James 1:2

When He said, "
Just believe"
When he said, "
Forgive their sins"
When He rose in the air
When He blessed them and promised to return
The Joy! The Joy! The Joy!
Is still here From 2,000 years ago
The Joy! Is still here
Waiting for His return
Oh! What a day that will be
The Joy!

Chapter 22

Peace

Recently I was encouraging and admonishing a friend of mine to receive the gift of peace.

"Peace I leave with you. My peace I give unto you; not as the world giveth, give I unto you. Let not your heart be troubled, neither let it be afraid." John 14:27

She was attacked severely with anxiety and sickness. She was unable to eat and her mind just ran away with her peace. Her body physically shook and she had hot and cold spells. What made it worse was she was trying to pray all the time so her mind was exhausted. The Lord revealed to me she was headed for a nervous breakdown. I saw how precious the gift of peace is and how difficult peace is to obtain if you strive. It's a gift given freely by the Father. Just receive!

We sought the Lord to show us what the problem areas were. She had taken care of her husband and children pretty much by her self since her husband's illness two years earlier. She was an organizer and a strong nurturer. She felt she was unable to get the nurturing she needed from the Lord. God spoke this to her:

"Be still and know that I'm God"! Psalms 46:10

He began to show her how to rest in Him and let Him love her and how to receive it. God told her to be totally quiet and tell her mind to obey and to empty her mind of planning and foretelling what tomorrow brings. She was to let her husband care for all matters of the house and children for a while and let family and friends help. She was to rest and have no plans. She fell asleep while we were hearing from God. She had not been able to sleep prior to that night. We prayed that she would enter into His peace and work at keeping her mind controlled.

Let us labor therefore to enter that peace of God..Hebrews 4:11

She asked for the gift of peace, the peace that passes all understanding. I felt the peace come. Her body stopped shaking and her temperature became normal. Breathing got deeper and she fell asleep. We all got sleepy and couldn't even talk or didn't want to disturb the peace. I saw how precious and wonderful God's peace is and how the world has nothing to compare with this. Jesus is the Prince of Peace! How fortunate I am to be His. I was bought for a price. I am not my own, but His!

Chapter 23

Suddenly of God

Twins

This is about a couple faced with a life or death decision that resulted in God suddenly coming to their defense.

In her seventh month the mother started having labor and contractions so they went to the hospital. An ultrasound showed a baby boy with head down, and a baby girl being breech. She was dilating and the doctor there wanted to do an emergency C-section right away. The Father, Craig stood up to this and said, "No, We are believing that God will be with us in this delivery. We will wait." This caused the Doctor to react in such a fearful, forceful way that Craig then knew for sure he would not allow his wife to birth under these conditions. They had to sign releases to get out of there. In the midst of having to hear the tirade of fear and negatives coming from the doctor their faith remained great. Craig knew to pray for him and he did. They called me to tell me of their time and I gave them some homeopathic pulsatilla tablets that would help to stop the contractions. She took them and the contractions would slow down and often stop altogether so she went to full term.

The day before I was to leave for Christmas to be with my family, the twins had still not come. I woke up one morning to unusual sunshine and clarity. I jumped out of bed wanting to call my couple and see how they were doing and whether or not anything was happening. I never expected them to go the full 40 weeks. Just as I was thinking all this, I was being reminded by the Lord of His faithfulness toward them who believe. Suddenly my couple calls. They are not in labor but just wanting to see me and talk to get some reassurance. They are still so full of faith. God was in control. I said I'd shower and be right over.

It was a beautiful drive. I sang and prayed. I had visions of Lisa having the babies but then doubt would try to come in. The day was so up-lifting it pushed all fear away. I arrived at their home to the sound of worship. Lisa and Craig were at the piano singing to the Lord. I knew I was in the right place. How Sweet and how peaceful the atmosphere was. All the children were at church with their grandparents so we were sitting around fellowshipping about this birth. Lisa looked great, huge, happy and very ready.

I noticed she moved around a lot on her chair continuing to adjust the pillows. She obviously wasn't comfortable but no signs of labor. We had a wonderful time talking about the Lord and His grace, mercy, births, life and kids. We talked about what to do when I left for my trip tomorrow. Craig was certain he had a peace. Two other midwives and an apprentice were coming but I had really wanted to be with them too. I just couldn't see me not being there for the babies and Lisa because it's not what the Lord had shown me earlier. As the day went on it seemed less likely I'd be at their birth. I decided to go and we went over details of the birth. Then Craig said Nancy would you check Lisa before you go. At first I thought, 'Why she's not in labor,' but I too wanted to know if she'd changed from two weeks ago.

So I said, "Yes" if Lisa wants to be checked." She did. We laughed about all the what ifs and then I checked her. She was 8 cm and bulging bag of waters, WOW. I praised the Lord and announced, "Honey you're in labor do you feel like pushing?" Suddenly everything changed. Power came with joy unspeakable. We called the other midwives. They were at another delivery so we told them to hurry. I couldn't imagine how she could be eight centimeters with a bulging bag of waters and two good sized babies, ready to come but not be in hard labor.

The midwives arrived in time and we all visited, ate, laughed and told stories. We played on their exercise equipment and waited. Nothing happened for hours. Now it's starting to get dark. We talked about what if we broke her water. We didn't have a peace yet. So we waited.

Lisa was having a few contractions so we had the equipment all set up and everything ready for the two babies. We had plenty of hands to help. We were prayed up and speaking the Word of God over these babies.

Lisa and Craig spent some private time in the bedroom together and you could hear them laughing and talking. It was very special. I still get excited thinking about what happened next. They called me in to check her and while I checked her, her water broke. It was clear and gushing with a Baby coming in it. We caught little Stephen and rejoiced. While the other midwives were checking the baby Lisa pushed again and nothing happened. We waited a minute then felt for baby. Two feet were tucked up high crossed over each other. We said go ahead and push. She did but nothing happened. We were all praying and rejoicing and then one of the midwives just reached up in and lifted a foot up and pulled. Tugged a little and out came little feet then body, crying, and beautiful. We all were laughing and rejoicing. Lisa looked relieved. We all sat there thinking "What just happened." It all happened so fast.

The first baby boy weighed 7 lbs 8 oz and the little girl was 8 lbs 2 oz. Lisa looked great nursing the twins, smiling. Craig was holding Lisa and grinning big, praising God. Craig prayed over his family and was so thankful. Thankful for the greatness of our Lord to save and deliver. They were truly blessed for their Faith.

We all cleaned up and the family came to see the twins. Craig had put a beef brisket on and it was ready. We ate sandwiches and then hugged each other good bye till next time.

"Suddenly everything was good"
Thank you Lord Jesus.
Suddenly! Suddenly!
Life is good!
Suddenly! Suddenly!
Life is bad
Suddenly! Suddenly!

He is here
Watch for him Listen!
He is near
He makes everything
Suddenly! He is here!

Chapter 24

The Bad Report

Don't believe the lie. When you first hear a thing or see a thing, always STOP, and turn to the Lord for help. This will train you to take the counsel of the Lord first, not the blaring circumstances. It is important to speak the word of God or the word of truth, over your situation, all the time. Do this even when things are good but especially if a bad report has come. Speak over your conception, over the growth of your baby, your pregnancy, over your birthing process and over your other children. Cover them with the word of God, the truth. If you are speaking doubt and fear, that will be hard to overcome. You have authority in the word as a child of God so remember that walking and speaking the word is covering your family.

For I will not be moved by bad tidings because
I have put my trust in the Lord. Psalm 112

I was at a birth of a young couple who had lost a baby just prior to this pregnancy and this was their fourth child. Lots of turmoil was going on in their family. Dad had lost his job, they were losing their home that they had just remodeled, their older boy was very troubled and on the streets, they had bills pressing them. Their life was a mess. We prayed a lot together and were excited about this birth so we planned. I get to her birth and she is in the hot tub, in hard labor. She labored there for several hours. Finally I asked if I could check her and see how she was doing. We went in and got the bed ready for the birth, she didn't really want to birth in the tub. I checked her for the dilation and baby's little butt was there. I looked around for the daddy and he was in the living room. He seemed kind of nervous and not very involved. I told him about the breech position of the baby and he said, "What do you do?"

I realized I was working alone here and I got really nervous. I considered going to the hospital, but baby was coming. I went back to the mom and she was on her hands and knees, I said, "Honey don't push till you absolutely have to." She said she would try. We were praying out loud, I was talking to the Lord about how I wasn't going to do this anymore. God laughs at me a lot. Next thing I know mom pushed and a head popped out. I couldn't believe my eyes. I yelled, "It's a head." Daddy had come in just prior to her pushing and we looked at each other, WOW! How does this work, how did baby turn that quickly? God is so good! Baby girl was born screaming, lively and healthy, Praise God!!

Chapter 25

The Lie

"The thief cometh not but to steal and to kill and to destroy; I am come that they might have life and that they might have it more abundantly." John 10:10

That's what the lie is, a thief that steals the blessings God has laid out for you. We need to start picturing this. Here is all God's blessing for you and the liar or lie comes and robs them. God says,

"They are yours, don't let the thief take them. They are yours, take them back, right now."

Because I know how much God loves me it is hard for the enemy to take things from me because I know they are mine, through Christ Jesus. This is especially true when it comes to babies. Babies are fearfully and wonderfully made. End of story, so stop the liar from robbing families, especially in the womb. Years ago a friend of mine Jane was pregnant and so excited. She traveled a lot with her work and just didn't think she would have anymore children, but God stepped in. Jane was pregnant and life took on a new sweetness. We were all excited and I started prenatal with her and planned a homebirth.

One day she called me very upset. She had been to the Doctor and they did an ultrasound and they told her the baby was all deformed and would surely die. I said, "That's a lie! Come see me and we will pray." She came over and looked terrible. I remember thinking this report could probably cause more damage than what is really going on. Who do we think we are, telling a pregnant woman all this stuff about her baby. This baby is hidden inside of her tucked away from the enemy. So, I prayed about this fearfully and wonderfully made baby and we cast all this bad report, out, out, out! I told her to speak what God says about her baby. I said, "If you don't know what He says, find out. Look in the bible, it is all there for you." I could tell she was feeling better and baby was kicking all over the place. We talked about what she should do about the Doctor wanting her to go to Texas to a specialist. I felt it was weird but I said, "God will show you what to do." She decided to go to Dallas, Texas and see these Doctors.

She went and we prayed. She had ten Doctor's taking care of her. She said it was ridiculous but she was speaking life and health over her baby all the time. She got so bold, she spoke it even to the Doctors. They were impressed. Well, they kept her for 3 weeks and set up for her to deliver there at the hospital. It broke her heart because we had planned such a wonderful birth but we couldn't find a way. They were even going to induce her but we prayed over the phone for her to go into labor on her own and she did.

They prepared her for the worst. Worst scenario was death and next was a mass in the baby's lungs and stomach, that was probably life threatening. So Jane went into labor and had a 4 hour labor. "Piece of cake", she said. A healthy baby boy was born with no problems. The Doctors were baffled and we rejoiced and thanked the Lord for His goodness and His word. We always felt bad about not getting to do the homebirth. I believe that was a robbery but there may have been a higher purpose like the Doctors getting to see the miracle of life in Christ.

Recently, at the pregnancy center a mom and her pregnant daughter of 4 months came in and were very upset. They had just come from an ultrasound and we're told the baby had black masses in the stomach and wasn't developing and may not live. I yelled, "What a lie." They did not know what to say to me because they so believed this bad report. We prayed and cast that report out and started speaking life and health to this fearfully and wonderfully made baby. I declared this baby would live and declare the works of the LORD! They dried their eyes and said, "Amen." and left.

About two days later I got a little worried but the Lord told me to hold on to the word of life. I went in the center the next week and heard all this commotion. I said, "What's going on?" This mom and daughter came running up dancing and yelling, "Everything is fine. They did another ultrasound and all is well." Bless the Lord!

Don't receive the lie, pray! Pray the word and if you don't know what word ask God to show you. He loves to give you wisdom and His word is wisdom. He will show you. Let God in when you get reports that change your lives, it's His life, go to Him and ask Him what you will.

if you abide in me, and my words abide in you, you shall ask what you will, and it shall be done for you. Herein is my Father glorified, that ye bear much fruit, so you shall be my disciples. As the Father hath loved me, so have I loved you, continue ye in my love." John 15:7-9

> I will always find a way
> Come up here and fly away
> Take my word and speak today
> I will always find a way
> Trust me child to keep your way
> Nothing can change my plan today
> Take my hand and follow through
> Take my love, I cover you
> Come up here and fly away
> I will always find a way
> Trust me child today
> I have made a way
> Nothing can change my way!

So, why do bad things happen? We are not perfect yet and God doesn't change. Why is it so hard for humans to admit we missed it or just didn't have all the truth. We are working on it. Keep working, keep asking, keep talking to God about it. We are on our way to perfect, if we're headed toward the Lord. Look up, spend time with Him and Satan's lies will crumble in the light of your love with the Father. I believe a religious spirit tells us that God failed us. Or worse yet, that God did that to us. Dear God, why is it so hard to recognize our own mistakes. To recognize when we are off the mark may be the ultimate humility. The Lord knows all this and wants us to just keep practicing hitting the mark, get up and shoot again. Take the word and apply it to every situation. Don't be afraid to fall or fail. You will get it, it's really God's word, He will get it for you. Keep shooting!!

Chapter 26

The Lions Den

The Lord said:

"I'll never leave you nor forsake you." Hebrews 13:5 "Saying, Touch not mine anointed and do my prophets no harm." 1 Chronicles 16:22 "When thou passeth through the water, I will be with thee; and through the rivers they shall not overflow thee; when thou walkest through the fire thou shalt not be burned, neither shall the flame kindle upon thee." Isaiah 43:2

I WALKED RIGHT INTO THE LION'S DEN! Right into the fiery furnace. I knew when I stepped outside of the Health Department guidelines and took people who were determined to be a high risk that I was walking into the Lion's den. I took a couple I knew were going to come close to God like they never had before and it just excited me and fascinated me to walk in to the lion's den.

Cheri and Matt are precious, they have four children and I felt immediate trust with them. I talked freely about the Lord and spoke to the Lord when we were together. Cheri had a C-section for her first birth and had done well with her last three. She had been at a birth of her friend several years ago with me. Her pregnancy was great and we had such fun getting to know each other. Cheri was really growing big, too big, and I realized we could have twins or polyhydraminos, which is too much water and could make for many complications. We all knew the risks yet we prayed and hoped for the best. I was pleading the blood of Jesus around them and me.

Cheri went into easy labor but unfortunately the baby's head was nowhere near the cervix or engaged. With so much water the baby was floating and which could cause problems with cord prolapsed or malpositions, (positions of the baby that aren't good for delivery). We prayed that baby would come down into the birth canal. I prayed her water wouldn't break until the baby came down. I stayed one day with them and contractions stopped so I went home.

The next morning Matt called and labor had started in earnest. Some bloody show was happening so we all got excited. I knew to really stand on the word of God for this baby and birth and didn't go right then.I especially stood on the following scripture:

"When thou passeth through the water. I'll be with you." Isaiah 43:2

Matt didn't call again until 5:30 that evening. Cheri was now having hard contractions and thought she was in transition. I arrived about 7 o'clock and they were relaxing, laughing and visiting with family.

Cheri was so relaxed I could hardly believe she was in labor. I checked her to see how dilated she was and got a real surprise. She was 9 cm. and a bulging bag of water totally filled the birth canal. This would normally be something to shout about but there was one problem. Where is baby's head? It was floating around nowhere near being engaged.

Oh God! I cry unto the mountain from whence cometh my help! His divine power has given me everything I need for life and Godliness, goodness and mercy forever. It was time;

"to go boldly into the throne room of grace that we may obtain mercy and find grace to help in time of need." Hebrews 4:16

I had a similar situation several years before. Mother ready to deliver but baby floating high up and not coming down because of too much water. At that birth we waited 6 hours for the baby to birth then finally we went into the hospital. I'll never forget the Dr. checking her and saying everything I knew only he said, "You made the right decision, she needs a c-section." I said, "Is there no other way?" He said, "No." He then proceeded to break her water the cord came down and they rushed her into the operating room. I always felt that this was wrong.

Yes we had a baby in a bad position but I knew God had a way for this. So, I told the family this story and I said in all conscience, "I can't call 911. Daddy, you have to make this decision." He promptly said, "I can't." So I turned to the Holy Spirit and I asked Him to show me how to do this. I know you have a way." Immediately I heard, "Have her squat and during a contraction feel if the head is coming down, if it is have her push a little and see what happens." I can still feel the flush in my face as I listened to the Holy Spirit with caution, not to get this wrong.

So we did just what the Lord said, as she squatted and felt the contraction I felt the head come down and she pushed. Two times we did this and on the second time baby Bonnie came flying out in a huge gush of water. I caught the baby, she was heavy and water flowed everywhere. We were laughing and crying and so was baby. I believe she was glad to be here.

Listening to the Holy Spirit is so important. I love listening now. I ask Him all kinds of questions. He is sent to help us. He is truth. Since this birth I have had to do this with several women who have had lots of babies with lots of water. Now during the pregnancy when I see lots of water I pray for the Father to decrease the water and call the water to be normal. I have seen this work too. God's handiwork is awesome!

Chapter 27

Laughter

"A merry heart doeth good like medicine," Psalms 17:22

"He that sitteth in the heavens shall laugh: the Lord shall have them in derision." Psalms 2:4

Laughter is an amazing tool or weapon, many times God uses me with laughter to bring the plans of the enemy down. I've seen the effects that the fire of laughter has upon the enemy. It brings confusion to the enemy. During the birth of Sammy, we had some fun moments and some intense laughter. It started when Bret called me to come over. Bea was in hard labor and it was about 3am. I lived on the other side of the mountain.

I arrived and Bea was lying on the bed with both her toddler and five yr old laying at the end of the bed in their little pajamas. I kept saying maybe we needed to move the kids but Bea was really in a place of work and intensity. She wasn't talking or looking at anyone, which told me she was close to birthing. Bea also gave off a sense that something was wrong. I tried to talk to her but she was really in her self, so I prayed everything was alright. I hadn't checked her because I just got there and I felt to leave her alone.

Bret was standing with a cup of coffee and we were just talking quietly when, Bea sat up and yelled, "Oh!" This startled Bret and I and we saw what looked like a huge bucket of water thrown on the kids. SPLASH! Both kids jumped up, crying and in shock, saying, "Why did mommy pour water on us." We were all laughing so hard, I couldn't believe I'd ever seen so much water.

The kids were just dripping, even Bea was laughing. Sammy, the baby, came flying out with a cord wrapped tightly around his neck. We couldn't get nervous or afraid for him because we were all laughing as I unwrapped and worked with Sammy. He cried and joined in the festivities, the two children were now laughing and it was a great time. To this day we still laugh about, the sibling water birth!

Another birth that laughter really helped was Tina's birth. Tina called me to tell me she was pregnant but in the hospital on total bed rest. Her blood pressure was amazingly high and the Doctor didn't know what to do. She had been in the hospital for weeks and everything was in a mess. Her marriage was hurting and she felt abandoned and all alone.

I was listening and then I just started laughing. I mean really laughing because I saw the enemy being lit on fire and running. It was so funny. I don't think I have ever seen anything as funny. I just roared with laughter and soon I heard Tina laughing. She rolled on her bed laughing very loudly. We laughed about the nurses seeing her, we laughed about her getting kicked out of the hospital, at the thought of being arrested for laughing, we were hysterical. She went on to deliver and all of her ordeals were healed. She just got dumped on during her pregnancy but laughter helped break the enemies attack. I believe laughter was her best medicine. God you are so good. Thank you!

Laughter in the Lord is very powerful. I have seen in the spirit where laughter breaks the enemy's back. It sets him on fire and pours out oil of joy. He can't stand because it causes such confusion. It causes the enemy to turn on himself. I've seen the enemy torn apart because of laughter, crying and begging to leave him alone and bring his demise.

Sometimes laughter is the only weapon that will stop the enemy in the situation you're in. In worship I laugh a lot at what the enemy is doing and it totally reverses the attacks and sets us in a heavenly place. I believe laughter is like love, if it is heaped on the enemies head it changes things. Try laughing at your bills. I dance on mine too. Try laughing when you feel like crying or your angry. My husband and I can hardly ever get mad at each other for laughing. We try to stay mad and just end up laughing. That is the Lord. Thank you Lord, for you are laughing at the enemy.

The voice of the Lord is upon the Waters
The God of Glory Thunders!

Chapter 28

All Creation Groans

for the manifestation of the sons of God. Romans 8:19

This couple, Lisa and Dave had 5 births and this was the sixth. They had always had easy wonderful births.

I arrived to a house full of joy and family. The mother was in good hard labor and seemed very close to giving birth. We waited, eating and talking, resting and praying. Finally she asked if I'd check her and see if she could push yet. She was complete and baby's head was right there. It was so joyous. Baby's birth was eminent. I said, "Yes you push whenever you feel like it. She said she didn't quite feel like pushing yet so we waited. After a while I said, "You just need to push anyway and she said, "I don't feel to push yet." So we prayed and continued to wait.

Finally, I felt desperate in my spirit and I began to groan. I put my head on her belly and groaned so Lisa started groaning. It was very compelling. I felt totally weird doing it but I had to groan. Suddenly she pushed and groaned too. Another push and then another and baby emerged. Big baby, full of life. We realized that the groanings of the Lord produce.

We have talked about this birth a lot and realized how important it is to do what the Lord is leading you to do. The mother said "I really had no push in me till I heard and felt your groaning. Then the Spirit of the Lord took a hold of me and I groaned and pushed. It was a wonderful feeling." I rejoice in His love for us. All creation groaneth for the manifestations of the sons of God. They named the baby Caleb, a son of God. This was a manifestation of a son of God, Caleb. He was a promise, a good report in the midst of giants. The promise came forth.

I attended another birth in the heat of the summer. Teah's water broke and I came over to help her labor start. It was horribly hot and they lived in a trailer with their mother and had no air conditioning. We literally sat with our feet in water and wash clothes on our necks. We had a lot of fun together but no baby yet. It was going on to 48 hours and there was no sign of labor. I felt like Elijah, watching for the cloud. It was in the night and I was trying to sleep but it was too hot. We were getting discouraged and starting to get fearful, knowing tomorrow we may need to go to the hospital. The thought of baby being in utero without the water made us all restless.

I couldn't go to sleep. I just laid there, crying out to God with my mind racing. A song floated by. One that my husband wrote years ago about; "The steadfast love of the Lord never leaves you, even though bees surround you, I cut them off in the name of the Lord. Nations surrounded me. I cut them off in the name of the Lord. The Lord is my rock and my deliverer!" This song would not stop so I finally went to sleep.

I had a dream that was so real. I dreamt that Teah's husband came in to wake me to tell me that Teah was crying and needed me. In the dream I got up and went to her. I had so much compassion on her that I fell over her pregnant tummy and cried out to the Lord. I groaned and I cried in tongues. Then I got up and went back to bed, the dream ended. Then, I was really being awakened by her husband. He said, "Teah needs you, she is upset." I got up went in and Teah was in a melt down. She was crying and saying, "This baby is never coming. I don't want to go to the hospital, please Nancy, help me."

I forgot the dream, but I fell over her tummy and cried out to the Lord to deliver her. I groaned and cried in tongues. Then it all seemed better so I went back to bed. I thought how odd to have a dream and then it is happening. I laid there for awhile singing that song and then I fell into a deep sleep only to be wakened by her husband again saying, "Hurry Teah is in labor." I ran into the room and there she was on hands and knees, pushing, baby was coming. I had nothing ready even though I had been there for two days. We laughed, we cried because God had heard our cry. He was delivering his little girls, she had a baby girl. Oh, what a wonderful God we serve. You never know what wonderful surprises He has awaiting you.

We are in dark times. The end times are here and groanings are of God. Groan when there are no words. Groan when nothing is in sight and you're desperate to the end. With compassion cry out to the Holy Spirit to help you with groanings that bring forth birth.

"For we know that the whole creation groaneth and travaileth in pain together until now. And not only they, but ourselves also, which have the firstfruits of the spirit, even we ourselves groan within ourselves, waiting for the adoption, to wit, the redemption of our body. For we are saved by hope: but hope that is seen is not hope: for what a man seeth, why doth he yet hope for? But if we hope for that we see not, then do we with patience wait for it. Likewise the Spirit also helpeth our infirmities: for we know not what we should pray for as we ought: but the Spirit itself maketh intercession for us with groanings which cannot be uttered. And he that searcheth the hearts knoweth what is the mind of the Spirit, because he maketh intercession for the saints according to the will of God. And we know that all things work together for the good to them that love God, to them who are the called according to his purpose." Rom. 8:22-28

For God is not unrighteous to forget your work and labour of love, which ye have showed toward his name, in that ye have ministered to the saints, and do minister. And we desire that every one of you do show the same diligence to the full assurance of hope unto the end: That ye be not slothful, but followers of them who through faith and patience inherit the promises. For when God made promise to Abraham, because he could swear by no greater, he swore by himself, Saying, Surely blessing I will bless thee, and multiplying I will multiply thee. And so, after he had patiently endured, he obtained the promise. Hebrews 6:10-15

You are the oak tree
You are the Love
Shading me Keeping me
Safe, in your love.
I can trust you
I can lean on you
Strong and sure
You are Like a live Oak
By the waters
Your love covers all.

Chapter 29

Casting Down Idols

Casting down imaginations, and every high thing that exalteth itself against the knowledge of God, and bringing into captivity every thought to the obedience of Christ. 2 Corinthians 10:5

I met this delightful family with 5 children. The husband is full of love and exuberance for life. His wife is very quiet, very sweet. I just loved them. We talked of the Lord and we fellowshipped a lot during their prenatal visits. We talked for hours about the Lord Jesus.

In the middle of the night I got called to their birth. She usually goes quickly so I hurried. It was an hour away but I found myself singing and praising God all the way. I hung out with them and slept for a while. It seemed early in her pregnancy for her to be birthing. I checked her in the morning and nothing was happening so I ate breakfast with them and decided to head home.

I got called again a couple of days later and went over there. Her labor kept starting and stopping. For 24 hours it just kept taking breaks. She was getting very tired and agitated. It was about 3 in the morning and I felt something was hindering this birth so I started really focusing on praying.

I ended up face down on the floor praying while everyone was sleeping. I was in their bedroom lying on the floor. I looked up as if Jesus was showing me something. It was a picture of the Mormon Tabernacle. I said, "What is that?" The Lord said, *"An idol"* I just started praying in tongues out loud. I bound it up and loosed the truth in this family. Within a half hour she was in hard labor and pushed twice and a little girl was born. We were all surprised.

One night I got a call from the husband, the daddy. He was so excited. He had met Jesus, The King of Kings. We talked a long time that night and he said he had always known something was keeping him from really knowing the Lord as his friend. He had found Jesus and now he knew he could go through anything. He knew the Lord was with him now and life had just begun. His whole family met Jesus after the father came to the Lord.

The next birth we did together was totally different. We sang, prayed, ate and laughed. When the baby came I was standing on her bed blowing the shofar. What a difference the fellowship of believers is. How awesome is the Lord who saves and delivers. Thank you Lord for this family.

Casting down idols and vain imaginations can be anything in your life that you hold onto that is bigger to you than Jesus. Even holding on to fear or pain of something that looms big in your life will twist your trust in the Lord. King David said:

"If there be any iniquity in me reveal it my Lord." Psalms 139:24

The Lord through the Holy Spirit has made a way for us to have the light of the word shine on these idols in our lives. Watching for places in our walk where we don't trust the Lord or we put more confidence in the things of the world. For instance, trusting medicine or doctors or our job, more than in Jesus' healing or His provision. Sometimes it's just as simple as watching more TV then spending time with our children or spouse or Lord. The idols in our life can change so we need to constantly keep a watch, or clean house so to speak.

Look around your house (life), from time to time and remove things that don't give a clarity of purpose or focus to your life. Sometimes we clutter up our lives and then when trials or tribulations come we can't even see clearly to stand against the enemy. Smashing the idols in your life will clear the way for following or even finding Jesus. The light of the word shines through you and will illuminate these idols or twists in your life so blessings can come and take over your life. In Deuteronomy chapter 30 God commanded blessings to over take us. Thank you Jesus!

Come down, you that loom higher than Me
Come down, off the throne meant for Me C
Come down, you thief, the world can't see
Come down, you thoughts not of Me
Come down, the strongholds, keeping you from Me
Come down, cast down, pull down, smash down, take down
You will be free! You will be free!

Chapter 30

Count It All Joy

My brethren, count it all joy- when you fall into trials and tribulations. James 1:1

How many times in life do you walk along and you seem to just fall into trouble. There is temptation to get worried, fearful, faithless, because of what you see. But God is big, so big He seems to be in my face. Pressing in on me to trust Him. He wants me to know that I am loved and nothing can by any means hurt me.

The story of this family's birth tried me and had me pressed hard in the Father's face. I am reminded that He is so Big. I marvel at how He loves to delight me and deliver me.

I had been seeing this couple at the pregnancy center and food pantry where I work. The mother to be had come in for diapers and told me she was pregnant and how she had wanted a home birth but had had so many difficult pregnancies she knew no one could take her. No doctor would ok her for a home birth. I laughed knowing she didn't know I was a midwife and I was touched by her desire for a home birth.

I listened to her stories of her other pregnancies. They ranged from placenta previa, where the placenta is over the cervix and the birth can't happen, for 2 birth's, to c-sections and 1 normal birth. I held onto the normal birth story. I continued to listen till I had heard: "I would love to have a home birth" for the tenth time. Finally I said, "I am a midwife. How much faith do you have? We can do this if you want." She cried, "Yes, I'd love to. You mean you'd come to our home?"

So then we began the pre-natal visits and got to pray and know each other. I really liked her and her husband and their big family. I was scheduled to do a home visit when I got a call one night that she was having pains. She didn't know if I should come. I felt I should go because I hadn't been to her home yet and it may take me awhile to find it.

When I arrived they were getting ready to go to the hospital. I said "Why? What is going on?" Her husband said she is in so much pain and is worried. I sensed everything was fine and suggested that I check her to see if she was in labor or not. They agreed and I checked her.

She was completely dilated and had a bulging bag of waters. I laughed and said, "You're having the baby. Relax and enjoy this because it is almost over." We ran around getting things ready. Her older daughter helped me a lot. We had such fun getting the bed ready. Just the excitement of birth, the anticipation of a baby coming was thrilling.

The heart tones were good and baby was lined up and ready to go. Mother was relaxing and even daddy didn't seem to be overly nervous. They had scriptures all over the house which were very comforting. All the children were up stairs playing. We were ready for baby's arrival.

I sat on the bed singing and laughing. The Day of the Lord was upon us. He was spinning love over us. His presence was all around us. Suddenly her water broke and I waited for her to feel the urge to push. She did and she pushed and pushed and kept pushing. The baby's head came out but she couldn't seem to push the rest of the baby out. I sensed shoulder dystocia. This is when the shoulders are stuck under the pubic bone and baby can't be born with out help.

We got her on her hands and knees and pushed. I pulled and I cried out for Jesus' delivering power. I did a wood screw maneuver where you put one hand on the babies back and the other hand on the babies chest up inside the vagina and you turn with both hands until baby pops out. All this needs to be done with the mother on her hands and knees. We did a lot of praying in tongues, commanding life and declaring baby come out in Jesus' name.

Baby flopped out on the bed, gray and lifeless. I began to speak life and massage baby ready to do CPR if necessary but Praise the Lord! Baby cried and cried and cried. He cried like he hurt, so I checked him out and his right shoulder looked uneven and he cried hard if I moved it. I knew I had to really pull on baby and on his shoulder to get an arm out. So I feared his collar bone was broken. His arm visibly hanging down, lower than the other arm.

I told his parents and they couldn't process all of that, they were just relieved baby was out and breathing. So we cleaned up and ran a tub and got both mother and baby in the tub. He was still crying. I felt so bad. I said, "We may have to go to the hospital to see about his collar bone. Then I heard the Father, God say, "Do you not Trust Me? I can fix his collar bone just like I gave him life." I said out loud, "Lord will you heal his collar bone and take his pain away? Thank you Lord. Thank you. Forgive me." Soon he was quiet and we rejoiced. We got them out of the tub and dried off and in bed.

I said, "Let's look at his collar bone." We looked and we couldn't remember which shoulder it was. We moved his arms over his head. Held his hand and no pain or crying. No difference in either arm. No arm was flopping down. He even moved his arms around and lifted them up on his own. Praise the Lord! God had healed him two thousand years ago and we believed him today and saw it. I've seen the family many times and baby is growing and normal. Praise God for his life and his healing.

In that short time of the birth, fear griped me more than once and I knew the family was fearful but our God is Good and He delights in the prosperity of His people. He loves us and He wants us to trust Him, to cry out, to command, and to have compassion even though we fall into trouble. We rejoiced and saw our Father's love. I continue to rejoice and so does the family. They received much faith that night and saw more of their Father then they ever had. God knew what was going on and He delivered them from all their fears.

And if we know that he hears us, whatsoever we ask, we know that we have the petitions, that we desired of him. 1 John 5:15

Perfect love casts out fear. 1John 4:18

I Am not afraid I Am not afraid
I Am bigger than anything you've ever seen
I Am not afraid
I Am greater than any thing you can believe I Am full of light
Shear bright white light
I Am beautiful to him that believes
You will see it
You will believe it
If you hold fast to me
I Am, all you need

Chapter 31

Asleep

An old granny midwife used to tell me about women that slept at the time of their birth and the midwives had to be careful or they would pull back the covers and find that the baby had arrived. I always wondered if I would see that. To have a baby come that easy seemed so wonderful. I had seen lots of times where we all got sleepy just as baby was coming. During that pushing stage there was like a blanket of sleep thrown over us and momma slept and so did I. But we always woke up to deliver the baby. These were special moments in peace and love. I try to cultivate that peace at births. I believe it eases the stress to baby allowing more blood flow to baby as he or she is born.

I was called out late one winter night to a birth for some dear friends. I had attempted to deliver with them a couple of years before but the baby came so fast that daddy delivered his little girl. I was happy for them and thankful everyone was alright but missed the precious labor time with them. So, this time I was really watching her closely to see any signs of labor starting.

I arrived at midnight and all the family were up. The children were excited and mom was in the tub. She was smiling and was so happy I had made it. Daddy was busy in the kitchen getting herbs on and hot water to sterilize scissors for cutting baby's cord. Music was playing softly praising God for His creation. I felt really happy to be here. I didn't feel a need to check her since she looked so comfortable in the tub. I pulled up one of the kid's stools and leaned on the edge of the tub adding warm water as she needed it.

Very little conversation took place. The music and the peace spoke for itself. The children eventually fell asleep on little beds dad had made for them. Dad brought a chair in and sat down. We mostly just sat looking at mom who by now was dozing off and on. I was real curious as to how far along she was but it just wasn't that important to know Considering how relaxed she was. I must admit I was thinking she must be early because I could hardly tell when she had a contraction. I just noticed her breathing a little deeper at times about three minutes apart. I could see baby moving and attempted several times to listen to heart tones with my fetal scope but it just seemed to take away from the serenity. So I leaned back to the edge of the tub and silently meditated on how good God is to make a way like this for baby and mom.

About two hours went by and now mother was sound asleep. I wondered if too much warm water would slow her labor down. Maybe I should insist she get out of the tub. That thought was no good since I knew she was too comfortable like this and maybe it was so early that she needed this precious time. Daddy and I smiled a lot not wanting to break the perfect silence. We felt a bond in peace for her and baby and we drew strength from each others' feelings of helplessness. For there was nothing we could do but watch a sleeping, beautiful pregnant mom.

I knew something special was happening but what was happening? Then I noticed a few bubbles coming from her perineum and then a little string of blood. I was shocked. She must be pushing now during a contraction so I watched her stomach and certainly she was pushing down but she was now snoring and quite loudly at times. We couldn't help but laugh silently. Now I was starting to get excited. What should I do? Pull the plug? Get her on to the bed? No. Just leave her alone, she's sleeping.

Soon the baby's head began to bulge out. I could see black hair and wrinkled skin. We are going to have this baby asleep in the tub and no one is going to say a word. I was so excited I could hardly stand it and papa and I did a lot of grinning and mouthing at this point. Mother never moved but slept perfectly at peace. I tried to talk to her but she only made some sleepy moans and it seemed to disturb her so I stopped. We got towels and bulb syringe ready. I did let the plug out because I chickened out and nobody stopped me. I wish now I would have left the water in. So I live and learn.

The baby's head came out and then his shoulders and then his whole body. Daddy and I we were at such an awkward angle it took both of us to pick baby up. Mother was still asleep and not appearing to be in any distress. Soon the baby cried and mother woke up and reached for her baby. Daddy handed baby to her and kissed her. She looked totally rested and aware of her baby. I lost it then. I cried tears of amazement and joy at what a fine birth. Baby was a boy and weighed eight pounds fourteen ounces, pink and lively. All the children woke up and were running around. I helped deliver the placenta in the tub and just washed everything down the drain. Easy, huh! Mom eventually got out of the tub and on to a soft clean bed where she nursed her new boy. She was lovingly looking over all his parts and features totally wide awake now.

Even as I sleep, you are there
Even when I wake , you are there
Everywhere, everywhere
You are there! I rest in thee*!*

Chapter 32

Overdue Babies

Danielle and Stephen have always been 3 weeks overdue which causes much distress. When we met I felt an immediate bond and we agreed together that God will make a way for them to have a joyous birth with no anxiety. I knew from then on all would be good. About a week from her due date Danielle started to go into labor we all got so excited but then her labor stopped. Oh how I wished we would have used castor oil when she started in but we felt she would go into false labor without birthing. I saw Danielle trying so hard to rest on the Lord but she was waning.

Lots of encouragement to stand on the agreement of the Lord for a joyous birth would bring us all back and then guess what. Yes, her water broke. We all rejoiced because she was just a few days past her due date. When I arrived I found the water to be green and labor real mild. I immediately asked the Father how were baby and this birth going to be? He said, "Joyous." Amen! That's all I needed to hear. I monitored heart tones a lot and labor was seemingly easy to me. Within 2 hours we had a baby girl.

Danielle's mom and friend Linda, Stephen and the two other older children were with her. Just after baby was born big sister, Abbey, woke up and wanted to see her baby sister. There was a tremendous feeling of peace and confidence that has great recompense of reward.

Half way through Danielle's birth, Tabitha called, another pregnant mom. She was 3 weeks early and just sure she was delivering any minute. I called another midwife, to see if she would go to Tabitha and cover till Danielle's baby came. After

Danielle's birth I drove at 3 in the morning from Berryville to Fayetteville to see Tabitha. I was tired but excited. When I arrived nothing much was happening and upon questioning found that all that day Tabitha had decided to have this baby. She went four wheeling, took castor oil and sat up all night telling herself she was going to have this baby tonight. I have to admit I was a bit perturbed. Her mother and sisters were there and everyone was hyped up and burrowed in for the duration. I sat for about an hour and realized I couldn't do this. I had work tomorrow and her cervix was thick and closed. I prayed for wisdom and strength. I felt to give her some labor tincture but I said, "I'm going to bed and went in and laid down.

I woke up at 6 and they were still sitting in the living room waiting for baby. I told them if she hadn't made progress I would leave for work. I was so sleepy and worn out the fun seemed to be gone. I checked her and much to my amazement she was 4 cm. and totally effaced. I got immediately encouraged and praised the Lord. He is so good. By 10 we had a baby boy and a very happy mom and dad and midwife. I found out later that she had a Doctors appointment that she really didn't want to go to. Oh. How strong willed we are but God is so full of grace. Thank you Lord!

Chapter 33

Birth Stories

The Winter Water Breaking Births

I've never seen anything like this. Tammy and John a very young couple that live near Missouri called one night right after an ice storm and her water had broke. They were so excited and they were staying with their family about an hour away from their own home. I was also an hour away from their home. Tammy was two weeks early and had been having pre eclamptic. Her blood pressure was rising so I prayed with them about bringing the blood pressure down and getting total rest and focusing totally on the Lord. He whose mind is stayed on the Lord is in perfect peace. I Also spoke to John about being the priest of his household and to take authority over Tammy's body and command it to line up with the word of God, which he did.

Later they went to the health department and the blood pressure was 110/70, very normal. Praise The Lord! So here we were having a baby quickly as I was to find out later. We decided to head to their house even though contractions had not started. I always ask the Lord to talk to me about the birth and prepare me for a blessing or a battle. He said, "It will be a very joyful and happy birth, to go and enjoy it." He also said I would make it which made me realize things may be rushed.

So off I went at 11 at night thankful it was not the night before since we had had a lot of ice that covered the trees and roads. The route I was to take wound through some of the most beautiful Ozark Mountains. So I praised the Lord all the way there and made wonderful time and arrived just as they arrived from their parents. I could see Tammy was in good labor. Her contractions had started once she got in the truck to ride home. She said they were hard and close even from the beginning and she felt she could push if they got any harder. I began thanking Jesus for His grace and sufficiently. I could feel the angels crowding in and the presence of His majesty. We all got quiet and were singing little songs to ourselves and we all had smiles on our faces.

I checked Tammy and found she was completely dilated and could begin to push. She was all propped up on pillows and relaxed like a flower ready to open. John was holding her hands and coaching her to breath. Hot packs were set up and applied to her perineum which she commented were wonderful. We laughed about making horse sounds to relax her mouth and shake her legs and arms out. Tammy said, "I didn't know this would be so much fun." Her mother and sister were in the kitchen making tea and watching the sterile instruments on the stove. They were excited with great anticipation.

Tammy began to push and soon we blew instead of pushing to take a slower more gentle approach to birthing the baby. She rested in between and smiled looking radiant and so relaxed. She said thank you Jesus after each blowing contraction. Within minutes we could see the hair. Oh, how excited daddy got. He told Tammy that we see hair so she put her hand down to feel baby's head and squealed in joy. The next push was little and then more blowing to let the body keep the perineum intact. She had perfect control. Out slid the baby's head, beautiful, round, little pinkish hair. Daddy helped lift baby to mother's stomach and looked to see what God had given them and announced, "It's a girl."

We praised the Lord and checked new little Tabitha over. She was a beautiful eight pounds and such a blessing. Momma had no rips or tears in her perineum and was feeling very fine. We all prayed over baby and mother and blessed this family, thanking God for a wonderful birth and life in Jesus.

Another Winter Water Broke Birth Story

Carli and Keith, a young couple who are spirit filled Christians so sweet and yielded to the Lord. Carli's water broke at 3 a.m. They called me about 6:30 a.m. to tell me, "No Lamaze classes tonight cause they were having a baby and would I like to come." I was surprised and a little shocked because they weren't due for 4 weeks yet. I immediately felt a peace and excitement and asked if any contractions were coming yet? No, But they would call me when anything started. So I went on to work, happy and praising the Lord for I knew today was a special birthday. About noon I really wanted to hear from them so I called. They were just hanging around calling folks and still very excited but no contractions. It was a rainy cold day so no amount of walking was going to help get things moving. I felt I should start praying. Sometimes contractions don't start in the time we need or so we think. Immediately the Lord spoke to me.

"You know she'll have contractions and the baby will be fine. Trust me. They will have a wonderful and peaceful birth with lots of joy."

God's voice always comforts me and sets me in a large place. I still wanted to be with them and see if I couldn't get things going. I called and asked them to get a fleets enema just in case we needed it. I told them to do some nipple stimulation and be prayerful. They were great. They were laughing and goofing off, telling me baby was active, the water clear and they were being very careful to keep clean and taking showers not baths.

Finally work was over and I couldn't stand it any longer. I kissed my hubby goodbye and headed to Bentonville about an hour away. When I arrived they were glowing. Carli was running around in just a tee shirt and undies. Actually they were Keith's and we all laughed about that. We ordered pizza and ate and talked about the Lord and how wonderful He has been in all our lives. Mike and Gail, their pastors, came by and we prayed together asking God to bring this baby tonight and thanking God for so much love poured out upon us.

Carli's mother called and seemed pretty concerned. She wanted me to do something to get things going. I did give Carli an enema after that. Carli did a lot of running to the bathroom but still no contractions. It was now 8:30 p.m.. and we were having a great time visiting and thanking Jesus for contractions. I went in the kitchen to do the dishes and I began to pray in the spirit and really Praise the Lord. I was delighting myself in the Lord when the Lord spoke to me, "You know in a twinkling of an eye contractions can start and everything will be ok. Believe in me." I felt so good. I imaged contractions starting and turned my total trust to God and no one else. I was content and I knew that I knew all would be good. But little did I know that within seconds they would be in labor.

"In a twinkling of the eye" Keith called out contraction! I yelled Praise the Lord! Yes, there is a great feeling when you have trusted God completely. Within a half an hour labor was fast and hard. Carli was throwing up and Keith was telling her how pretty she was and we were laughing and cutting up. I lay down to sleep for awhile but I just listened to the birthing sounds and listened to the Lord. He wooed me in an out of sleep. Keith came in and said I think it may be getting close.

I checked Carli and she was 5cm. We all sat in blissful silence as we watched Carli breathe. She was having a little bit of trouble due to the contractions being so hard. She started to cry and got grouchy so I started praying for the Holy Spirit our comforter to come and help her and to surrender totally to Gods delivering power. She sighed a big relief and fell asleep. We we're all just amazed and the greatest peace came over us. All we could say was the peace that passes understanding was upon us and we were in awe.

Carli soon had to push and when she did she laughed and said, "Oh! This feels so good. We asked Jesus to be our labor coach and carry this baby out as the scripture says in Isaiah; He carries us from the womb and bears us up in old age." Carli smiled with each contraction and soon she felt the baby's head and squealed thanking Jesus. She totally trusted God for this delivery. We all felt a peace and joy and crying at one point. She had perfect control so when a contraction came, she pushed the baby out and daddy put his hands around the little round head and out slipped a little girl. Kaila Lil, we all were crying and laughing praising the

Lord for His wonderful and mighty delivering power. What a mighty God we serve. She didn't tear or have any trouble with the placenta or bleeding. We had a great time cleaning up and taking the herb bath and looking at baby. It was 2 a.m. and the fellowship was great as we shared about how good God is. Every good and perfect gift is from above. This is true unity of the spirit and fellowship. God is good!

The Third Winter Water Birth

The third winter water birth happened all within four days. I had three babies in four days and all their water broke. The moon was almost full and the closest to the earth it will be till 2029 wow! Rick and I were at our dear friends Ron and Carlene's. We had been in town all day looking for pianos for Carlene. I had my beeper on so I was very comfortable about being out and about. We went to their house to watch a movie. We had great fellowship but Rick felt we should go. Usually it's me wanting to get to bed early but I was wanting to stay and visit. We got home and on my answering machine was a message that Michelle's water had broke. I immediately called and Anna, Michelle's mom, told me her water broke at 9'o'clock and it was now 10:30 and contractions were hard.

They had been beeping me but no answer. I was shocked but so thankful God was in control and I hoped I would make it. I Praised the Lord all the way there. Ice and snow had come earlier but now all was clear. I felt such a joy that I get to be a part of all this love and faith. I asked the Lord how all would go since their last birth was a caesarean section and I was stepping out in faith to do this birth but the Lord assured me all was well and joy would be full.

I arrived and Michelle was complete and could push whenever she was ready. Soon a beautiful baby girl arrived. Everyone was so happy, they had five boys and everyone was rejoicing. Thank you Jesus for Your

Life, Your promise, and Your power. Glory to God!

Rachel And Her Great Big Family

I have delivered eight babies for the Hampton girls and they were always an experience. God is teaching all of us a lot with this family. Rachel's first baby Victor was a horrendous birth. I believe now that there was repentance and healing needed and we discovered that when the baby arrived totally white and limp, very lifeless.

I remember the morning of Victor's birth the Lord showing me while I was in morning prayer that He would never leave me no matter how dark it got. I thought at the time something was near but had no idea till I saw this baby. I cried out to the family to pray. I started to catch the baby and in my spirit I was praying but nothing seemed to be going anywhere. It was as if I were sinking into a dark black pit.

I said call 911 and get me the oxygen. It got so dark I felt faint. Then I remembered the Lord's words that morning.

"I will never leave you no matter how dark it gets."

I yelled, "Yes Lord"! Faith instantly came and I felt it go into the baby's tummy. It was like lightening and his tummy got pink and I started rejoicing and he coughed and looked around totally pink and crying. I looked down and Rachel was hemorrhaging. I prayed:

"And when I passed by thee and saw thee polluted in thine own blood. I said unto thee when thou wast in thy blood. Live; yea Live."
Ezekiel 16:6

At the same time I heard Rachel crying out to God to heal her baby and she was saying, "I want this baby Lord, let him live, I'll name him Victor". We all cried and I realized I should have prayed with Rachel about the circumstances of her pregnancy and whether or not she wanted this baby. I repented as I felt we all did in the room. We were totally humbled by God's presence and now there was Holiness. We were on Holy ground. We were all rejoicing when the EMT's came in. They looked like people from another land. They took one look at the baby and said all is well here and just left. I felt they were shocked by some strange presence ,who we know to be the Friend that's closer than a brother. The King of Kings, the Mighty God in our midst. We rejoiced and loved on each other and the baby, I stayed about seven hours that day just basking in the presence.

Well after a birth like that I have to admit I wasn't thinking about the next time and here we were. Rachel was pregnant again. I did figure out that Victor had a very short cord and as he descended into the birth canal Rachel's placenta was getting pulled very hard. This explains her intense pain that was very out of proportion to the labor happening. Baby was being compromised and her placenta was tearing from the uterine wall causing much bleeding and pain. God repaired it all, yet I knew there we needed to explore any sin to be forgiven and I was going to pray this time and fear God and be wise.

So immediately I talked with Rachel about her last birth and that there was no father present and this birth was happening out of wedlock also. Rachel was preparing to get married so we prayed together and agreed to pray constantly for guidance in her life and in the direction of the birth.

I was beeped at 9 o'clock that morning. I felt joyous and ready. Her water had broke so I called Carly, another midwife, and hurried over to the birth. On the way I had wonderful fellowship with the Lord. He assured me all was prepared and to trust Him using my faith. Stand for joy and it would abound, and that He was in charge.

When I arrived, all the sisters and their mother were there. Much peace and love was present. Rachel appeared to be far along so Carly and I got things ready and we checked her. First she was only a tight four centimeters and her water was green. Not thick pea green which would not have been good but green. I looked at Carly and she looked concerned. I watched a few contractions and they seemed very hard, harder then they should be. I checked with the Father and what He wanted me to do. He had a very happy sound in my spirit and said all will be fine. We got her up to the bathroom and she was miserable. I just felt so bad for her I instinctively began to pray. I heard God say, "What's best?" I said,

"Best, yes! What's best here?" I prayed out loud, "Lord let the water's become clear and ease her pain."

I looked at the faces around me and they were questioning. We got her back on the bed and I started to Praise the Lord for His word and presence. Everyone got really peaceful accept Rachel who was far away and in intense pain. I felt to check her again and I started to cry. She was complete and when I took my glove out there was pink clear fluid running out. Three pushes later and little Theadra was born. I delivered her and only pink fluid came up. No heavy bleeding and a tight uterus. What can I say? God is so good. We all laughed, ate and visited together.

Rachel said: "Can I take my herb bath with her. I didn't get to last time." So she was up and walking around smiling and Praising the Lord! We still pray for her and her boyfriend since he wasn't able to be there. It just happened too fast. I don't know how their relationship will turn out but we are praying and I know God is in the situation. I'm learning that He will work His perfect will in us when we give God the problems and keep open to His direction. This can take a lot of time but patience and long suffering will pay off.

Nellie and Les's birth

It was fast and joyous. She called at noon and was at work feeling like something was happening. She decided to go home and lay down. I figured she'd sleep awhile but she just couldn't rest. About 2 o'clock I started thinking strongly about her and called her. She said the faint cramps were about 3 minutes apart. I said I'll be right there. I notified my boss and I was on my way. All the way there I felt I may not make it. Finally I asked the Lord what was going to happen. He said:

"You'll make it."

I said, "I might make it, but will she be delivered already?"

The Lord laughed and said, *"You'll make it to the delivery."*

I instantly relaxed. One word from the Lord and it's settled. I got there and Nellie was standing in the door. I saw her belly-still pregnant! Then I wondered if this wasn't a false alarm. I had just checked her the day before and she wasn't dilated very much. I watched her for awhile and her family came. We decided to check her. She was complete and a bulging bag of waters. We got so excited praising the Lord. We were wanting for the water to break. Finally Nellie said, "Why don't we just break it. I don't feel like anything is happening. Let's get things going." So, I broke the water and a couple of pushes and out came Savannah, 10 pounds 2 ounces, with beautiful black hair. She was sucking and pink when she arrived. Praise God He allowed me to make it. I know God holds on to babies and IS in total control. Thank you Lord.

The Two Births In One Day: Hurray!

Doug and Janie were overdue and getting anxious. I called to see how they were doing and she said there was a lot of pressure and cleaning out happened earlier in the week. She didn't have much appetite and some infrequent contractions. We had had a lot of rain and the rivers were flooding. Spring was here and I decided to go for a ride down the scenic 23 S highway. It was gorgeous. New green trees, red buds and Dogwoods that look like popcorn blooming in the trees. Sun shine with a mist and even fog up high. The river was running fast, muddy brown but unusually pretty next to the new trees and red buds. There were lots of yellow forsythia's too. I felt so close to God looking at His creation and knowing new life was coming. Little did I know two new lives were coming. I felt exceptionally good.

I asked the Lord to talk to me. He immediately said;

> *"It's going to be a joyous birth and easy. Relax and enjoy looking at My day and rejoice."*

I began to sing and shout in tongues, worshipping God and His Hosts. His Greatness is Greatly to be praised! The streams were flowing down the mountain in places I've never seen before. It was such a spiritual ride. Living waters washing away all the muck and mire. Love covers a multitude of sin. Oh, how God loves us.

I arrived to see Janie and little John at the door. It was a good sight. John was three now and so cute just like his dad. I remembered seeing him at his birth. I love it that I never forget a birth only some names though, I need work on that. We visited and I checked her. She surprised me with 4-5 cm. and about a 0 station. Wow! We're going to have a baby soon.

We laughed and remembered all the births. I had helped with five of her births and now number six. I said; "Are you having any contractions now"? She said, "Not lately." So we proceeded to decide what to do. I knew I could probably get labor started with an enema but Janie said no, she wanted the kids fed and in bed and she reminded me that she always has the babies at night. I decided to leave. The drive home was just as good as the coming. I arrived home and talked with Rick for awhile excited about how beautiful it was up on Burney Mountain and started to make dinner.

The phone rang, it was Doug. Janie was in labor and it was fast. I knew this was good. I kissed Rick and off I went to that pretty drive and I said all the scriptures I could remember. Faith cometh by hearing and hearing by the word of God. I felt my spirit man growing.

Janie was at 7 cm. and a bulging bag of waters. We praised the Lord for awhile and I scurried around for teas and getting instruments boiled. The kids were all there and so helpful and full of questions and awe. Doug and I hugged. We hadn't seen each other since the last birth. What a shame that we get so busy we can't visit more and fellowship. Karen, a good friend of Janie's and mine arrived. We were going to have fun now.

It was about 6 o'clock now and everything was ready so we just sat and waited. Her contractions were getting closer and more intense. Her water broke and she needed Doug now. He held her hand and she squeezed so hard we laughed about it. Karen held little John and we all got little chairs (kid's chairs) and sat around quiet during a contraction and talking between. Here comes the baby. Cold rags for mom's head and hot for her bottom. A pan to throw up in and olive oil for massage to perineum to help stretch everything. The kids were good and so helpful. Just as the head began to show, John came up on the bed and sat by his mom. He had a look of true empathy. The black headed baby was almost here.

Another push and actually a blow and baby swooshed out. We "blow the baby out" by blowing with the mouth. This keeps mom from pushing at the end because it's too much for the perineum and causes it to tear. All the kids were up off their little chairs with mouths open and looks no one can describe. Here was little John holding baby's hand and saying, "This is my baby brother." It was time to look and yes, it was a brother. Mom and dad were crying and we were all rejoicing for God is good! We visited some more, got Janie and baby in the tub and back to bed. We were all sitting around laughing at how this was not at night. I said I could get a good night's sleep, when my beeper went off. It was Larry's voice. Another baby was coming. Yahoo! Another adventure with God. Oh how I love this birthing. Everyone helped me get it together. Lots of hugs and kisses and off down the mountain to Berryville and another birth.

Julie and Robby

Such a young couple. So much patience and love went into this couples birth and life. By the time baby was to come we were overdue and I was starting to wane as far as patience. Let patience have her perfect work and she did. I was never so happy to see a baby get here. Surprisingly, June did very well. She is the only person I have ever put my hand over her mouth to keep quiet. She had a fisherman's yell and out of nowhere she would bellow at Robby. We were thankful the birth was during the day and neighbors were riding their lawnmower's around. I truly know God has a sense of humor. I truly loved this couple but they were very trying. I learned peace comes from God and how He is peace and each one of us tries the Father like this. I am grateful for this couple and pray they learned as much as I have. Thank you Father for baby Krista.

Martha and Jorge

Their baby arrived in the night. Rick and I always go out to the lake on the weekends but this weekend we felt to stay home. It was a nice thing since they called about 8:30 p.m. She said she was in hard labor and they had a ways to travel from Prairie Grove where they are migrant workers for a family. I have been fortunate to deliver two of their five children. They are quiet people but Jorge shared a lot during this birth. We had a lot of time to visit since Martha wasn't really in hard labor yet.

I've learned that long births may be just for the reason to get a sharing time and the Lord does much with this special time. Jorge had only been to school several months. It was too costly for his family to send him. His brother who lives with him and who I also get to help soon with a baby, showed Jorge how to read and write. He had no teaching on numbers so Jorge always keeps a calculator handy. Martha went into good labor the next day after we all got a good nights sleep. A 7 lb. baby boy, Salbador was born about 2:30 p.m. with no problems. Momma and baby were ready to go home an hour later. Rick and I went out to the lake and swam. It was beautiful and the peace and joy after a birth are to be remembered when we are in the storm. He's grace is sufficient.

Backup Surprise

June and Dr. Jerry were doing a birth for a friend and asked if I would back them since they both wanted to go to a counseling weekend for married couples. The counseling weekend fell on the weekend of her due date. I met with the couple and we really hit it off. They were really open people. They did not know the Lord but they were open to His love. We did several prenatals together and Lorain, the mother, expressed to me she felt better about me being there than the original plans. I prayed and wondered how it would turn out.

Jerry, being a doctor, had given Lorain prescriptions for medications like demeral and phenergan. I knew I would not give these yet they are planted in Lorain's mind and could present a problem. As it turned out Lorain went into labor Saturday of the weekend they were gone.

Her contractions started at 6:30 a.m. I had seen her the night before and she had flu like symptoms that I felt could be labor. Her baby was still floating and cervix was 1cm about 30 % effaced. So it didn't surprise me that she went into labor. I talked with Chris, her boyfriend, about it possibly taking awhile, so find some outlets for Lorain. Things like bathing, walking, relaxing, or cooking. Her contractions were close together and I've noticed when they are close in the beginning you need to relax and get your energy to change and get regular, harder, longer, and further apart pains that let you rest in-between.

About noon Chris called and said they were really getting strong and were 3 minutes apart so I felt I should go even though I felt it was still early. There may be something I can do to help her energy to get focused. I arrived and she was in the tub. They have a very creative house that was her mother's. Lorain's mother died last year from cancer at a young age. Lorain was very talkative about her mom. Most of her mom's friends were going to help Lorain during the birth. The bathroom was very spacious with lots of windows looking out on the trees. It was a beautiful day. There were two overstuffed chairs in the bathroom and I just settled into one and enjoyed the breeze from the windows and chatted with Lorain.

She looked radiant and the bath definitely helped the contractions not to hurt. Lorain shared with me that she was really glad I was there and she didn't want a lot of distraction around her. There were a lot of phone calls from friends and her mom's friends. It was now very peaceful. I slept a little in the chair and just enjoyed the peace.

Later I checked her and she was 2 cm and about 90 % effaced. Lorain mentioned, when do I get something for pain. I looked her in the eyes and said I will never give you those drugs for pain because I will use love to help you by massaging, praying, positioning, bathing, walking, and getting your eyes off the pain. Lorain looked at me with shock. "You're not going to give me anything for pain?" I knew she was thinking this lady is nuts and I'm in big trouble. I smiled and said, "Trust me. I've never needed to use drugs. They don't help with the pain they just drug you so you can't tell anybody you hurt and they hurt baby and slow the labor. You are doing fine. Focus on your breath relaxing you and opening the cervix.

After this rude awakening the contractions got really hard. We all started massaging her legs and back putting pressure on her tailbone and back area. She really liked the massage. Then back to the tub. This seemed to help the most. Around 6:30 p.m. I checked her again and she was now about 4 to 5cm but the baby's head was high and just not getting engaged but she had a bulging bag of waters. Lorain felt if the bag would break she'd feel better but I knew the head had to come down or the cord could come down. So I prayed and waited.

About 9 o'clock I decided to try pushing since the cervix was completely effaced and elastic like a rubber band and about 8cm but the head high. Maybe pushing would bring that head down and break the water and we'd have a baby. The minute we started pushing she looked better. She had more energy and with it the contractions got real centered and manageable. It took an hour before the head came down and water broke. The heartbeats were good and the water was clear. I tried to keep her from pushing so the cervix would disappear but she had tasted pushing and now just wanted to push each time.

Two and a half hours of pushing got baby out and daddy caught that little slippery baby boy Marley. The video of the birth was great. We all sat and ate pasta and watched even though it was 1 a.m.

Mom looked great. No tears, no heavy bleeding, and hardly any weakness. We got her up and in the tub for her herb bath with baby. Baby was so cute with fat little cheeks and real rosy skin. He loved the bath. We all enjoyed this birth and couldn't get over how we did so good. One of her friends said you didn't even need drugs and Lorain winked at me and said. "She wouldn't give them to me anyway, and then laughed." God is good. He was there in a very real way. I tried to stay totally in His presence so that they could witness His love and peace with them.

Ice Storm Births

Babies always want to come in storms, especially ice storms. We were having a big dance recital at the rink and it started to snow then ice. It was a mess with people trying to get out of the parking lot. We were praying that everyone would get home safe. It didn't occur to me that any babies might be planning on coming. We had decided we couldn't get home so we bedded down at the skating rink where the party was. About midnight the phone rang and it was Iris, who I had helped with two of her births. They were not pregnant but a couple they met in Michigan were. They were uncertain of what kind of birth they wanted and Iris and her husband had told them about their wonderful births so this family said "Lets go to Arkansas and birth." So here they were in Arkansas in the middle of an ice storm and she is in hard labor. I had never met them, it was her first baby, and it was terrible weather. God gave me a great peace. I believe it was more for them since the realization of birth was now starting to scare them. I reassured them all night till I heard in her voice they really needed some physical assurance. I tried to get out of the parking lot and it was a no go, so I called the sheriffs office. They were great, they sent an officer over to take me to the birth. He had four wheel drive plus chains, so off we went. We had a great time talking and he was so excited to go to a birth. We finally arrived and she was still laboring but was very close. The officer wanted to stay just in case we needed a ride to the hospital but we assured him we would be fine, everything was normal and baby was coming. Baby did come and we all rejoiced. What a night, what a wild time but baby was here and the ice was already melting, so beautiful the trees are glistening with ice on them in the bright sunlight. What joy and how sweet, the story for the sheriffs office, the family and how sweet our God is who sees everything and knows what it takes. Thank you Lord!

Rainy Night, Low Water Bridges

I always am ready to leave a birth and get on home when I know all is well. It had been raining all day and all night. The birth was long but wonderful. A baby girl was born and mom was nursing and dad was sleeping and I felt it was time to fly home. I got in the car and wasn't far from my house but I had to cross a low water bridge no matter which way I went so I took the shortest route. It was 3 a.m. and I was ready to hit the bed.

I really never thought about water rising or any worries because I was still high on God's birthing. He is so wonderful. I was literally singing in the rain and talking to God about all the little birth things I don't understand like why does it take so long for the cervix to open with some women and what a miracle birth is, when woe! I am on a low water bridge that I can't see and water is rushing over the banks and road and now my car has stalled.

The van was rocking with the force of the water and all I could think about was how stupid to get yourself in this position at 3 in the morning. Yicks! What do I do now? I cried out o God! I turned the car lights off so I didn't run the battery down and now it was pitch black, oh now I'm getting nervous, Oh, God where are you? What should I do? Suddenly I knew I needed to get out and get help. I opened the door and water came rushing in, thank goodness it was fall and the water was still warm. I stepped into the knee high water and felt for the road, yes, I am on the road. I held onto the van until I couldn't any more and then I carefully felt for the road and pushed thru the water to the bank.

I got on the road and began to walk to find a house. I was singing loudly because the water was loud rushing through the creek bed and I was scared, so I had to be louder than my thoughts. Suddenly, some horses in the field startled and whinnied and ran, I yelled, "Oh God" and ran too. What a sight that must have been to people with night vision. I was now nervous about dogs or anything I couldn't see. I was thinking of crazy things like why didn't I go to births with a partner someone to drive me. Then the Lord reminded me that He is my partner and He is with me and all will be fine, this is ok and my van we'll be fine and I'll be in my bed soon.

I was having trouble believing this when right in front of me was a house. I stopped and assessed the situation looking for dogs and wondering if I should knock at the front door. It looked too formal and rarely used so maybe the back porch would be better. I could see it and it felt more neighborly, how silly I thought, just go to the door. As I reached for the screen door a man said, "Hey, what's ya doin?" I jumped and said, "My van is stalled on the bridge and it's flooding." He opened up the door and reached for something on the shelf and said, "I have some stuff here that will help ya, come on, I'll drive us over."

I couldn't believe what was happening but it was wonderful. I took a good look at him as he came out the door. He had on overall's with one side unsnapped and no shirt, boots on and he grabbed his hat on a hook by the door. He never turned a light on and I didn't see or hear anybody else around. I started to get a little scared, just because of the unknown and getting in a truck with a guy I didn't know but then I felt kind of happy and giddy, excited about this situation, what next? So we hopped in the truck and off we went down the road. I told him about the horses scaring me and he laughed. He said, "It's pretty dark out for a young women to be walking about I bet you scared those horses silly."

Now we were at the creek and the van was still there, thank God! He jumped out and said, "You stay here," he walked into the water and opened the door, popped the hood and sprayed some stuff in the carburetor. He got back in the car and turned the engine on and drove carefully to me. I was just amazed. I said, "How did you do that"? He laughed and said be careful now and go home and get to bed." I laughed a little at how simple the fix was. I thanked him and said, "You have no idea what a blessing you are." I jumped in the car and started home. I sang and cried and had goose bumps all over me from excitement.

I was excited to tell Rick about the night and this guy. Who was he, how weird, how sweet. I got home and Rick was really worried. He was hoping I didn't have trouble crossing the low water bridge and said he had been up praying for several hours. I told him the story and we could hardly get back to bed. The next day we took a ride over to the low water bridge to see how it looked and to stop by and thank the nice man, who helped me. We drove over and the water was still high, we marveled at how faithful the Lord was to send help and keep me and my van safe. We saw the horses I startled and then went to the house of the man who helped me.

The house was completely abandoned and we drove around it and then in the driveway. It was obvious no one had lived there in awhile. Who was the man who helped me and where was he? We sat for awhile wondering what had really happened. All I knew was that it did happen and here I am, alive and well, even happy and astonished that I had gone through a night like last night. So do angels drive trucks? God is so amazingly funny, thank you Lord!!!

Chapter 34

Newborn Care & Babies

1. Watch baby's color. It should stay pink. If gray call on Jesus and your midwife or Doctor. If blue, hold baby up to your face and look baby in the face, this clears airway letting baby breath.

2. If baby starts to turn yellow just check out how active the baby is. If crying and eating, good, then probably all is well but if yellow gets in whites of eyes or in palms of hands and bottoms of feet call your midwife and she'll problem solve.

3. Baby should have a bowel movement and urinate within 48 hrs. First stool will be blackish and after breast milk comes in a couple of days it will be yellow and runny. Baby will have a bowel movement about eight times a day but sometimes not for a day. It is not unusual for a baby to be irregular. If so try to massage baby's tummy. Sometimes pampers soak up urine so it is hard to prove baby has peed.

4. Baby will sleep a lot and you might worry that baby is not breathing. Just watch baby's color. If pink and warm all is ok.

5. Crying all night or fussing is probably because days and nights are mixed up. You will have to try to keep baby awake during the day by bathing or taping feet. Sometimes nothing works so just take a good nap with baby and stay up at night praying. Spending time with the Lord and baby is good but don't let this get you weary. Just adjust your schedule. If your milk has not come in yet and baby is not letting you rest. Try a little sterile water or weak formula.

6. When nursing, be sure and lay baby flat to you. Put baby tummy to tummy and keep trying to put whole areola in baby's mouth. When baby gets a good hold let baby nurse for about 5 to10 minutes then switch. When baby gets breast milk completely out of one side before going to the next, the breast will feel limp or baby will get fussy. This nursing out each side completely avoids mastitis {a breast infection, where milk stays to long in the breast and gets it infected}. If baby is having trouble, let baby find its own way. Sometimes just relaxing and singing over baby clears the air. Momma needs to be relaxed to allow baby to find his way to the breast, to the latching on. Asking the Holy Spirit to help you immediately helps.

7. Fennel tea, a little beer or hops, or mother's milk tea are all good for increasing milk supply. Plus nursing as often as baby needs will increase milk and bring your milk in faster, less engorgement.

8. Baby should have a PKU test in about 3 to 8 days. This can be done at the Health Dept. Baby can be checked over by them or soon after birth with a family Doctor or Pediatrician.

9. Get a good baby book before baby comes this will avoid a lot of worry and unnecessary running around worrying, giving place to the enemy. The bible is a great baby book, everything in it applies to your baby and you.

10. Don't forget to sing to your baby and pray over baby. Let the Lord be your guide. Talk to your baby about the birth that you just had together and comfort baby if it was a hard journey. Babies!!! What gifts from God!

"Every good and perfect gift is from above, and cometh down from the Father of lights, with whom is no variableness, neither shadow of turning. Of his own will begat he us with the word of truth, that we should be a kind of firstfruits of his creatures." James 1;17-18

This is what birth is all about. That baby, so beautiful, so complete, so loved, longed for, cherished and truly the Lord's reward.

I remember the first birth that I saw Jesus in the eyes of a baby. The mom and dad were friends of mine. We had met by phone. They had called to see if they could meet us, they had heard about us and they lived in Kansas but wanted to come to Arkansas. We invited them to stay with us while they hunted for a house. We took care of their little baby Zach. They did move here and we became great friends, their second baby was born in a little log cabin on our pastor's farm.

It was a beautiful day and the women from our fellowship were there and the men were outside, Rick had taken Zach for a walk. We all were having so much fun singing and helping Tina when she got ready to push. She just pushed a couple of times and I heard her say, "He's pushing his way out." Out he came and while his dad was holding him, I looked into his big blue eyes, WOW! I saw God in his eyes, I didn't want to let go of him. God was so peaceful and clear, it all made sense, so sweet, all in a baby's eyes.

I am praying for women because they are losing the blessing of birth. Because we are such a comfort minded society and we want things fast. Women are not taught or conditioned to wait or endure. Faith is not in the picture, although I think it takes way more faith to go to a hospital today. Birth is God given and women can grow up in birth and they will birth many things for their husbands, children and kingdom. I guess you could say it is our art, our anointing. Women were created to birth. It is an honor to birth God's creation.

We can find more of ourselves through God birthing a deep groaning for more of HIM. There is more, go deep, go deeper! Resist the temptation to find a way out of birthing. Instead find your way in. The Lord will help you and you will find Him in birth. God and God alone is the deliverer. There is nothing in birth to fear. Everything about conception, pregnancy, labor, and raising a child is joy, a surety from God that He is with us. The Lord watches over us and keeps us. We are rooted and grounded in His love. Trust the Lord, let Him deliver you, and the host of heaven will surround you with love.

I love the following story of Mary and Elizabeth, in reading this ponder the time they were in. Ponder the event of an immaculate conception, the friendship, the womanhood, the life, culture and time in history. Ponder the faith, courage, love, and joy. Realize the prophecy, the Praise, the surrender, respect, authority, intercession, heritage, and the journey of destiny. Do you see yourself? My hope and prayer is that you do see yourself because those verses are a picture of our Kingdom walk today. Mere women were chosen to make the way for the Savior our King of Glory. We have been chosen today to make that way for the Savior to be shared and embraced by those we meet. God has a plan for us, it is good. Thank you Jesus!!

"And she spake out with a loud voice, and said, Blessed art thou among women, and blessed is the fruit of thy womb. And whence is this to me, that the mother of my Lord should come to me? For, lo, as soon as the voice of thy salutation sounded in mine ears, the babe leaped in my womb for joy. And blessed is she that believed: for there shall be a performance of those things which were told her from the Lord. And Mary said, My soul doth magnify the Lord, And my spirit hath rejoiced in God my Saviour. For He hath regarded the low estate of His handmaiden: for, behold, from henceforth all generations shall call me blessed. For He that is mighty hath done to me great things; and holy is His name. And his mercy is on them that fear Him from generation to generation. He hath shewed strength with his arm; he hath scattered the proud in the imagination of their hearts. He hath put down the mighty from their seats, and exalted them of low degree. He hath filled the hungry with good things; and the rich He hath sent empty away. He hath holden his servant Israel, in remembrance of His mercy; As He spake to our fathers, to Abraham, and to his seed for ever."
Luke 1:42-55

My life My life
My life is hid in you
You have plans for me
Sometimes only you can see
My life My life
Is so full of you

So Complete, so sweet
Life in you!

Scriptures For Strength

These Scriptures are to give you strength when you need it.

1. For we walk by faith and not by sight. 2 Corinthians 5:7

2. Neither be ye grieved; for the joy of the Lord is your strength. Nehemiah 8:10

3. For out of the abundance of the heart the mouth speaketh. A good man out of the good treasures of the heart bringeth forth good things. Mathew 12:34

4. God has commanded blessings on me. Deuteronomy 28:8

5. Whosoever shall call on the name of the Lord shall be delivered. Joel 2:32

6. For without faith it is impossible to please God. Hebrews 11:6

7. For God has not given us a spirit of fear but of power, and love, and a sound mind. 2 Timothy 1:7

8. For He hath strengthened the bars of thy gates. He hath blessed thy children within thee. Psalms 147:13

9. He shall not be afraid of evil tidings. His heart is fixed. Trusting in the Lord. Psalms 112:7

10. For I the Lord your God hold your right hand. It is I who say to you Fear not I will help you. Isaiah 41:3 11. It is well with my soul. Philippians 4:7

12. And ye shall serve the Lord your God and he shall bless thy bread and thy water; and I will take sickness away from the midst of thee. There shall nothing cast their young nor be barren in thy land; the number of thy days I will fulfill. Exodus. 23:25

13. The spirit of the Lord is upon me. Because the Lord hath anointed me to preach good tidings unto the meek; he hath sent me to bind up the brokenhearted, to proclaim liberty to the captives, and the opening of the prison to those who are bound; To proclaim the acceptable year of the Lord and the of vengeance of our God; to comfort all that mourn; To appoint unto those who mourn in Zion. To give unto them beauty for ashes, the oil of joy for mourning, The garment of praise for the spirit of heaviness that they might be called trees of righteousness, the planting of the Lord that he might be glorified. Isaiah 61:1-3

14. Blessed be the Lord my strength who teacheth my hands to war and my fingers to fight; My goodness and my fortress; my high tower and my deliverer; my shield and he in whom I trust who subdueth my people under me. Psalm 144:1-2

15. Tust in the Lord with all thine heart and lean not upon thine own understanding. In all thy ways acknowledge Him and he shall direct thy paths. Be not wise in thine own eyes; fear the Lord and depart from evil. It shall be health to thy navel and marrow to thy bones. Proverbs 3:5-8

16. Seven times a day do I praise thee because of thy righteous ordinances? Great peace have they who love the law and nothing shall offend them. Psalms 119:164-165

17. They shall not labor in vain nor bring forth in trouble; for they are the seed of the blessed of the Lord and their offspring with them. And it shall come to pass that before they call I will answer; and while they are yet speaking I will hear. Isaiah 65:23-24

18. But be glad and rejoice forever in that which I create; for behold, I create Jerusalem a rejoicing, and her people a joy. Isaiah 65:18

19. Before she travailed, she brought forth; before her pain came, she was delivered of a man child. Who hath heard such a thing? Who hath seen such things? Shall the earth be made to bring forth in one day? Or shall a nation be born at once? For as soon as Zion travailed she brought forth her children. Shall I bring to birth, and not cause to bring forth? Saith the Lord. Shall I cause to bring forth

and shut the womb? saith thy God. Rejoice with Jerusalem and be glad with her all ye that mourn for her. That ye may nurse and be satisfied with the breasts of her consolations; that ye may drink deeply and be delighted with the abundance of her glory. For thus saith the Lord: Behold, I will extend peace to her like a river and the glory of the nations like a flowing stream; then shall ye be nursed. Ye shall be borne upon her sides, and be dandled upon her knees. As one whom his mother comforteth, so will I comfort you and ye shall be comforted in Jerusalem. And when you see this your heart shall rejoice and your bones shall flourish like an herb; and the hand of the Lord shall be known toward his servants and his indignation toward his enemies. Isaiah 66:7-14

20. And he said unto me. My grace is sufficient for thee; for my strength is made perfect in weakness. Most gladly, therefore, will I rather glory in my weaknesses that the power of Christ may rest upon me. Therefore, I take pleasure in weaknesses, in necessities, in reproaches, in persecutions. in distresses for Christ's sake; for when I am weak then am I strong. 2 Corinthians 12: 9-10

21. Be not afraid it is I. John 6:20, Mt. 14:27, Mk. 5:36, 6:50

22. Faith cometh by hearing and hearing by the word of God. Romans 10:17

23. Be not wise in thine own eyes; fear the Lord and depart from evil. It shall be health to thy navel and marrow to thy bones. Proverbs 3:7-8

24. Trust in the Lord with all our heart lean not upon your own understanding. In all thy ways acknowledge him and he shall direct thy paths. Proverbs 3:5-6

25. Love covers a multitude of sins. 1 Peter 4:8, Proverbs 10:12

26. Behold, the Lord's hand is not shortened that it cannot save; neither his ear heavy that it cannot hear. Isaiah 59:1

27. As for God his way is perfect; the word of the Lord is tried; he is a buckler to all those that trust in him. Psalm 18:30

28. Faithful is he who calleth you who also will do it. 1 Thessalonians 5:24

29. And being fully persuaded that what he had promised he was able to perform. Romans. 4:21

30. He staggered not at the promise of God through unbelief: but was strong in faith giving glory to God. Romans. 4:20

31. My counsel shall stand and I will do all my pleasure: I have spoken it. I will also bring it to pass; I have purposed it, I will also do it. Isaiah 46:10b. 11b

32. So that we may boldly say, The Lord is my helper and I will not fear what man shall do unto me. Hebrews 13:6

33. And this is the confidence that we have in him that if we ask any thing according to his will he heareth us. And if we know that he hear us, whatsoever we ask, we know that we have the positions that we desired of him. 1 John 5: 14-15

34. When thou passeth through the waters I will be with thee; and through the rivers, they shall not overflow thee: when thou walkest through the fire, thou shalt not be burned; neither shall the flame kindle upon thee. Isaiah 43:2

35. Cast not away therefore your confidence which hath great recompense of reward. For ye have need of patience that after ye have done the will of God ye might receive the promise. Hebrews 10:35-36

36. Casting all your care upon the Lord for he careth for you. 1 Peter 5:7

37. Be careful for nothing: but in everything by prayer and supplication with thanksgiving let your requests be made known unto God. And the peace that passeth all understanding shall keep your hearts and minds through Christ Jesus. Philippians 4:6-7

38. And we know that all things work together for good to them that love God. To them who are the called according to his purpose. Romans 8:28

39. When I am afraid I will trust in thee. In God I will praise his word. In God I have put my trust; I will not fear what flesh can do unto me or what man can do to me. Psalms 56:3

40. And I said, Oh, that I had wings like a dove! For then would I fly away and be at rest. Psalms 55:6

41. Trust in him at all times ye people; pour out your heart before him. God is a refuge for us. Psalms 62:8

42. Every good gift and every perfect gift is from above and cometh down from the Father of lights with whom is no variableness neither shadow of turning. James 1:17

43. This is the work of God that you believe on him whom he hath sent. John 6:29

44. This is the entire Psalm 119. Many of these verses I have used in times of need. It is chock full of blessings.

Blessed are the undefiled in the way, who walk in the law of the Lord. Blessed are they that keep his testimonies, and that seek him with the whole heart. They also do no iniquity: they walk in his ways. Thou hast commanded us to keep thy precepts diligently. O that my ways were directed to keep thy statutes, then shall I not be ashamed when I have respect unto all thy commandments.

I will praise thee with uprightness of heart, when I shall have learned thy righteous judgments. I will keep thy statutes: O forsake me not utterly. Wherewithal shall a young man cleanse his way? by taking heed thereto according to thy word. With my whole heart have I sought thee: O let me not wander from thy commandments.

Thy word have I hid in mine heart that I might not sin against thee. Blessed art thou. O Lord: teach me thy statutes. With my lips have I declared all the judgments of thy mouth. I have rejoiced in the way of thy testimonies as much as in all riches. I will meditate in thy precepts and have respect unto thy ways. I will delight myself in thy statutes: I will not forget thy word. Deal bountifully with thy servant that I may live and keep thy word. Open thou mine eyes that I may behold wondrous things out of thy law.

I am a stranger in the earth: hide not thy commandments from me. My soul breaketh for the longing that it hath unto thy judgments at all times. Thou host rebuked the proud that are cursed which do err from thy commandments. Remove from me reproach and contempt; for I have kept thy testimonies. Princes also did sit and speak against me: but thy servant did meditate in thy statutes. Thy testimonies also are my delight and my counselors.

My soul cleaveth unto the dust: quicken thou me according to thy word. I have declared my ways and thou heardest me: teach me thy statutes. Make me to understand the way of thy precepts: so shall I talk of thy wondrous works.

My soul melteth for heaviness: strengthen thou me according unto thy word. Remove from me the way of lying: and grant me thy law graciously. I have chosen the way of truth: thy judgments have I laid before me. I have stuck unto thy testimonies: O Lord, put me not to shame. I will run the way of thy commandments when thou shalt enlarge my heart.

Teach me O Lord the way of thy statutes; and I shall keep it unto the end. Give me understanding and I shall keep thy law; yea I shall observe it with my whole heart. Make me to go in the path of thy commandments; for therein do I delight. Incline my heart unto thy testimonies and not to covetousness. Turn away mine eyes from beholding vanity; and quicken thou me in thy way.

Establish thy word unto thy servant who is devoted to thy fear. Turn away my reproach which I fear: for thy judgments are good. Behold, I have longed after thy precepts: quicken me in thy righteousness. Let thy mercies come also unto me O Lord even thy salvation according to thy word. So shall I have wherewith to answer him that reproacheth me: for I trust in thy word. And take not the word of truth utterly out of my mouth; for I have hoped in thy judgments. So shall I keep thy law continually for ever and ever. And I will walk at liberty for I seek thy precepts.

I will speak of thy testimonies also before kings and will not be ashamed. And I will delight myself in thy commandments which I have loved. My hands also will I lift up unto thy commandments which I have loved; and I will meditate in thy statutes. Remember the word unto thy servant upon which thou hast caused me to hope. This is my comfort in my affliction: for thy word hath quickened me.

The proud have had me greatly in derision: yet have I not declined from thy law. I remembered thy judgments of old O Lord; and have comforted myself. Horror hath taken hold upon me because of the wicked that forsake thy law. Thy statutes have been my songs in the house of my pilgrimage. I have remembered thy name O Lord in the night and have kept thy law.

This I had because I kept thy precepts. Thou art my portion O Lord: I have said that I would keep thy words. I interrupted thy favor with my whole heart: be merciful unto me according to thy word. I thought on my ways and turned my feet unto thy testimonies. I made haste and delayed not to keep thy commandments. The bands of the wicked have robbed me: but I have not forgotten thy law.

At midnight I will rise to give thanks unto thee because of thy righteous judgments. I am a companion of all them that fear thee and of them that keep thy precepts. The earth O Lord is full of thy mercy; teach me thy statutes. Thou hast dealt well with thy servant O Lord according unto thy word. Teach me good judgment and knowledge for I have believed thy commandments.

Before I was afflicted I went astray: but now have I kept thy word. Thou art good and does good: teach me thy statutes. The proud have forged a lie against me: but I will keep thy precepts with my whole heart. Their heart is as fat as grease; but I delight in thy law. It is good for me that I have been afflicted; that I might learn thy statutes. The law of thy mouth is better unto me than thousands of gold and silver.

Thy hands have made me and fashioned me: give me understanding that I may learn thy commandments. They that fear thee will be glad when they see me; because I have hoped in thy word. I know O Lord that thy judgments are right and that thou in faithfulness hast afflicted me. Let I pray thee, thy merciful kindness be for my comfort according to thy word unto thy servant. Let thy tender mercies come unto me that I may live: for thy law is my delight.

Let the proud be ashamed; for they dealt perversely with me without a cause: but I will meditate in thy precepts. Let those that fear thee turn unto me and those that have known thy testimonies. Let my heart be sound in thy statutes that I be not ashamed. My soul fainteth for thy salvation: but I hope in thy word. Mine eyes fail for thy word saying; When wilt thou comfort me? For I am become like a bottle in the smoke; yet do I not forget thy statutes.

How many are the days of thy servant? When wilt thou execute judgment on them that persecute me? The proud have dogged pits for me which are not after thy law. All thy commandments are faithful: they persecute me wrongfully; help thou me. They had almost consumed me upon earth; but I forsook not thy precepts. Quicken me after thy loving-kindness; so shall I keep the testimony of thy mouth. For ever O Lord thy word is settled in heaven. Thy faithfulness is unto all generations: thou host established the earth. and it abideth. They continue this day according to thine ordinances: for all are thy servants.

Unless thy law had been my delights. I should then have perished in mine affliction. I will never forget thy precepts: for with them thou hast quickened me. I am thine save me; for I have sought thy precepts. The wicked have waited for me to destroy me: but I will consider thy testimonies. I have seen an end of all perfection: but thy commandment is exceeding broad.

O how love I thy law it is my meditation all the day. Thou through thy commandments hast made me wiser than mine enemies: for they are ever with me. I have more understanding than all my teachers: for thy testimonies are my meditation. I understand more than the ancients because I keep thy precepts. I have refrained my feet from every evil way that I might keep thy word. I have not departed from thy judgments: for thou host taught me.

How sweet are thy words unto my taste! Yea, sweeter than honey to my mouth! Through thy precepts I get understanding: therefore I hate every false way. Thy word is a lamp unto my feet and a light unto my path. I have sworn and I will perform it that I will keep thy righteous judgments. I am afflicted very much: quicken me O Lord according unto thy word. Accept I beseech thee, the freewill offerings of my mouth O Lord and teach me thy judgments.

My soul is continually in my hand: yet do I not forget thy law. The wicked have laid a snare for me: yet I erred not from thy precepts. Thy testimonies have I taken as an heritage for ever, for they are the rejoicing of my heart. I have inclined mine heart to perform thy statutes away even unto the end. I hate vain thoughts: but thy law do I love. Thou art my hiding place and my shield: I hope in thy word.

Depart from me ye evildoers: for I will keep the commandments of my God. Uphold me according unto thy word that I may live: and let me not be ashamed of my hope. Hold thou me up and I shall be safe: and I will have respect unto thy statutes continually. Thou host trodden down all them that err from thy statutes: for their deceit is falsehood. Thou purist away all the wicked of the earth like dross: therefore I love thy testimonies. My flesh trembleth for fear of thee; and I am afraid of thy judgments.

I have done judgment and justice: leave me not to mine oppressors. Be surety for thy servant for good: let not the proud oppress me. Mine eyes fail for thy salvation and for the word of thy righteousness. Deal with thy servant according unto thy mercy and teach me thy statutes. I am thy servant; give me understanding that I may know thy testimonies. It is time for thee Lord to work: for they have made void thy law.

Therefore I love thy commandments above gold; yea above fine gold. Therefore I esteem all thy precepts concerning all things to be right; and I hate every false way. Thy testimonies are wonderful: therefore doth my soul keep them. The entrance of thy words giveth light; it giveth understanding unto the simple. I opened my mouth and panted: for I longed for thy commandments. Look thou upon me and be merciful unto me as thou uses to do unto those that love thy name.

Order my steps in thy word: and let not any iniquity have dominion over me. Deliver me from the oppression of man: so will I keep thy precepts. Make thy face to shine upon thy servant; and teach me thy statutes. Rivers of waters run down mine eyes. because they keep not thy law. Righteous art thou. O Lord. and upright are thy judgments.

Thy testimonies that thou host commanded are righteous and very faithful. My zeal hath consumed me because mine enemies have forgotten thy words. Thy word is very pure: therefore thy servant liveth it. I am small and despised: yet I do not forget thy precepts. Thy righteousness is an everlasting righteousness and thy law is the truth.

Trouble and anguish have taken hold on me: yet thy commandments are my delights. The righteousness of thy testimonies is everlasting: give me understanding and I shall live. I cried with my whole heart; hear me O Lord: I will keep thy statutes. I cried unto thee; save me and I shall keep thy testimonies. I prevented the dawning of the morning and cried: I hoped in thy word. Mine eyes anticipate the night watches that I might meditate in thy word. Hear my voice according unto thy loving-kindness: O Lord. quicken me according to thy judgment.

They draw nigh that follow after mischief: they are far from thy law. Thou art near. O Lord; and all thy commandments are truth. Concerning thy testimonies I have known of old that thou hast founded them for ever. Consider mine affliction and deliver me: for I do not forget thy law. Plead my cause and deliver me, quicken me according to thy word. Salvation is far from the wicked: for they seek not thy statutes. Great are thy tender mercies O Lord: quicken me according to thy judgments. Many are my persecutors and mine enemies; yet I do not decline from thy testimonies. I beheld the transgressors and was grieved; because they kept not thy word. Consider how I love thy precepts: quicken me. O Lord. according to thy loving-kindness.

Thy word is true from the beginning and every one of thy righteous judgments endureth for ever. Princes have persecuted me without a cause: but my heart standeth in awe of thy word. I rejoice at thy word as one that findeth great spoil. I hate and abhor lying: but thy law do I love. Seven times a day do I praise thee because of thy righteous judgments?

Great peace have they which love thy law: and nothing shall offend them. Lord, I have hoped for thy salvation and done thy commandments. My soul hath kept thy testimonies; and I love them exceedingly. I have kept thy precepts and thy testimonies: for all my ways are before thee. Let my cry come near before thee O Lord: give me understanding according to thy word. Let my supplication come before thee: deliver me according to thy word.

My lips shall utter praise when thou host taught me thy statutes. My tongue shall speak of thy word: for all thy commandments are righteousness. Let thine hand help me; for I have chosen thy precepts. I have longed for thy salvation. O Lord; and thy law is my delight. Let my soul live and it shall praise thee; and let thy judgments help me. I have gone astray like a lost sheep; seek thy servant; for I do not forget thy commandments. Psalm 119

Glossary

Anterior lip - An anterior cervical lip occurs when the presenting part is not positioned correctly upon the cervix, causing unequal pressure that results in unequal dilation

Bloody Show - cervix starting to open, blood vessels break causing slight pink or red blood in mucus.

Blood type- husband's blood type and mothers blood type need to be compatible especially important if mother's is negative.

Braxton-Hicks -uterine exercises, tightening of uterus, usually not painful sometimes called False labor

Bulging Bag of Waters –the bag holding the amniotic fluid bulging due to contractions, or labor.

Cervix - The narrow neck-like passage forming the lower end of the uterus

Doula - a woman or man who provides non-medical support to other women and their families during labour

Effaced - cervix thinning

Episiotomy - is a surgical incision used to enlarge the vaginal opening to help deliver

False Labor - uterine contractions that don't get closer together in timing

Hard labor -contractions that are close and hard and opening the cervix, usually at the transitional phase.

Hematocrit or Hemoglobin and glucose random or fasting - testing for iron in blood and sugar or glucose in blood.

Hemorrhaging -heavy bleeding, like a faucet turned on.

Hepatitis B -Infection in mother can be given to new born but can be treated successfully if baby is treated within 12 hours of birth.

Herb Bath -bath for after the delivery of placenta, helps heal the vagina and soothes the body. Herbs used: comfrey leaf, uva ursi, shepherds purse.

In Position -head down and engaged, ready for delivery

Labor Tincture -usually black & blue cohosh, helps labor progress.

Meconium - baby bowel movement in utero this usually causes the green fluid

Pap smear -swab of mucus off of cervix

Perineum -inside vagina

PKU -test for a rare enzyme deficiency which can result in brain damage and death.

Placenta previa -placenta is attached near or completely over the cervix, keeping baby from being born and or hemorrhage.

Polyhydraminos- large amount of water in amniotic bag

Pre Eclampsia - condition in pregnancy that is caused by stress on organs, producing high blood pressure, spilling protein in urine, and edema.

Rhogam shot -keeps you from producing your own permanent Rh antibodies and prevents your blood from recognizing the baby's blood cells as foreign. Rhogam is to be given with in 72 hr. of giving birth, it keeps your next baby from danger. Given because the mother and father's blood types were incompatable

Shoulder dystocia- This is when the shoulders are stuck under the pubic bone and baby can't be born with out help.

Station- position of baby in pelvic area, above or below pubic bone.

Titer if RH negative- a blood test can be taken to see if your body is building up antibodies against this pregnancy.

V-back -vaginal birth after a c-section

VDRL -venereal disease screening

Woods screw maneuver -a maneuver you do when a baby is in pelvic shoulder dystocia, baby's shoulders are stuck under the pubic bone and you can twist or rock baby from under the bone while applying pressure to pubic bone, thus freeing the baby.

Made in the USA
Middletown, DE
07 April 2016